Books by Clive Egleton

THE EISENHOWER DECEPTION (1981)

BACKFIRE (1979)

THE MILLS BOMB (1978)

SKIRMISH (1975)

THE BORMANN BRIEF (1974)

SEVEN DAYS TO A KILLING (1973)

THE JUDAS MANDATE (1972)

LAST POST FOR A PARTISAN (1971)

A PIECE OF RESISTANCE (1970)

The Eisenhower Deception

Clive Egleton

THE EISENHOWER DECEPTION

Atheneum New York 1981

Library of Congress Cataloging in Publication Data

Egleton, Clive.
    The Eisenhower deception.

    I. Title.
PR6055.G55E5   1981   823'.914   80-69397
ISBN 0-689-11127-4

This book is for R. A. E.

1956

Wednesday, October 3 to Thursday, October 4

1.

George Deakin stared at the log fire and was sorely tempted to hurl his notebook into the flames, a gesture which, although understandable in the circumstances, would have been wholly out of keeping with his usually placid disposition.

An acknowledged expert on the Middle East, Deakin had spent eight years in the Persian Gulf working for an oil company before joining the Special Operations Executive in Cairo late in 1940. After the war, he had stayed on with the British Middle East Office until 1950 when somebody in Whitehall had decided that he was just the man to head the Arabian Department at 54 Broadway near St. James's Park. Less than four months ago, that same anonymous somebody had moved him to the Russian desk to sort out the mess Kim Philby had left in his wake. From the moment he had assumed his new appointment, Deakin had felt he was singularly ill-equipped to hold down the job and now, on Wednesday the fourth of October 1956, that nagging doubt had been reinforced by James Hedley.

Had he been asked to gauge how far the Soviet Union was prepared to back Nasser in the Suez Canal dispute, Deakin could have dashed off a lucid synopsis in less than an hour, but in Hedley's case, it was harder. In fact, assessing his reliability in the absence of any corroboratory facts was well-nigh impossible. If previous case histories were anything to go by, agents who were picked up by the AVH were either quietly liquidated or put behind bars for a very long time. But not Hedley. Arrested in Budapest late last Saturday night together with a number of Hungarian dissidents, he had merely been held in solitary confinement for four days and then served with an expulsion order. Such lenient treatment was unheard of and Deakin naturally wondered what he'd done to deserve it.

"This Miklos Petki," he said abruptly, "the man who invited you to have supper with his friends Judit and Zoltan Mikes. How long have you known him?"

"Just under two years," said Hedley. "I met him through the Hungarian Writers' Association. Being a foreign press correspondent," he smiled, "I was invited to attend one of their debates. Petki was detailed to look after me."

."Why?"

"Because he could speak a little English." Another smile. "Petki is a very engaging character. The more I saw of him, the more I was convinced he was a valuable source of political information. The intellectuals who belong to the writers' association are a pretty outspoken bunch."

"Was Petki outspoken?" Deakin asked sharply.

"No, he just told me what his colleagues were thinking."

"He could have been spreading disinformation, couldn't he? I mean, we know Petki is a liar, don't we? That supper party on Saturday, for instance. Instead of the small intimate gathering you'd been led to expect, you found yourself embroiled in a political meeting. Isn't that so?"

Hedley stifled a yawn. Deakin had already taken him through his story in some detail, but apparently there was no satisfying him. With his rounded shoulders, sharp black eyes, hooked nose, and leathery skin, Deakin reminded him of a vulture. He behaved like one too, stripping the flesh from the carcass until the bones were gleaming.

"Are you tired?" Deakin asked softly.

4

Tired was an understatement. With little or no sleep for the past four days, he had endured a 160-mile drive from Budapest to the Austrian frontier, a rapid change into another car, and then on to Vienna airport and a BEA flight to London. At Heathrow he had faced a barrage of questions from the waiting reporters before his bland escort from "The Firm" had smuggled him out of the airport via the freight area into yet another car to face a very different kind of interrogation at Burnham House. Of course, compared with the stark interrogation room in the AVH headquarters on Andrassy Street, the library at Burnham House was pure luxury. There were floor-to-ceiling bookshelves crammed with leather-bound volumes, heavy velvet drapes in the windows, a log fire burning in the grate, and the sort of comfortable leather armchairs usually found in a London club. There was also one other major difference between the two establishments: measured against George Deakin, the AVH major who'd questioned him in Budapest had been a rank amateur.

Hedley sighed. "What do you think?" he said.

"I think we should talk about this political meeting." Deakin consulted his notebook and then looked up, a wintry smile on his thin lips. "Tell me about it once more."

Hedley shifted in his chair. "As I said before, suddenly there were two rows of chairs in a semicircle in front of me and Judit Mikes was inviting her guests to question me."

"You thought it was a propaganda exercise?"

"It certainly looked that way. One of them—a reporter, I think—had his notebook ready, and Zoltan opened the proceedings with a tricky question: he wanted to know if we and the French were going to invade Egypt. I said we wouldn't."

"Oh yes? And why was that?"

Hedley smiled wearily. Asking a man to give his views was an old trick. It enabled an interrogator to assess the attitude of the person he was questioning. If a man showed the wrong attitude, it meant he'd either been brainwashed or turned around.

"Okay," he said, "if that's what you want. As near as I can

5

remember, I told them that if we were to invade, the Egyptians would undoubtedly sink blockships in the Canal, which would pose a serious threat to our vital oil supplies, especially as the rest of the Arab world would probably side with Nasser. I also said the British economy was in no condition to weather a run on the pound and that this would be one occasion when the Americans would refuse to bail us out. I pointed out that it was election year in the United States and President Eisenhower wanted to remain in the White House for a second term. Since his advisers had gone to a lot of trouble to present him as a man of peace, they were not going to allow us and the French to rock the boat. . . . Do I pass?"

Deakin ignored the bait. "Then the instructor from the military academy jumped to his feet, asked if the Americans really meant it when they said they would support any nation in the cause of freedom, and you said—?"

"I said, 'Look at what they did in Korea.' "

"At which point you were handed a copy of their manifesto?"

"Which called for the withdrawal of all Soviet troops stationed in Hungary."

"A somewhat dangerous piece of paper," Deakin observed.

"Lethal would be a more accurate description." Hedley felt another yawn coming on and cupped a hand over his mouth. "At least that's how I saw it when the AVH broke into the apartment and took the lot of us down to Andrassy Street for questioning."

"Yes, the AVH . . . they had more than enough evidence to put you on trial but they let you go. I wonder why?"

"They didn't know I was working for MI6, if that's what you're worried about," said Hedley. "My cover was still intact."

"If you say so."

"I do say so. Look, this is my theory. Khrushchev simply didn't want a show trial at this particular time—against the dissidents *or* me—and simply told them to drop it. He's already removed Matyas Rakosi from power because he was a hard-liner and he doesn't want Prime Minister Gerö to go down the same road. The Poles have been giving him a hard enough time

6

recently without having a repeat performance from the Hungarians. So, they let me go."

Deakin masked his thoughts behind an impassive expression. The story was too glib, too pat, each piece interlocking with the precision of an all-too-simple jigsaw. He thought about what he knew about Hedley. He was a loner, thirty-two years old, single, and without family ties, his father dead, his mother living in Toronto. Commissioned into the King's Own Yorkshire Light Infantry after six months' service in the ranks, Hedley had served with the Forty-ninth Division throughout the campaign in Northwest Europe. The last nine months of his service had been spent in Palestine where he had been employed as an intelligence officer at GHQ. He had spent the next three years at Brasenose College, Oxford, studying modern languages, and joined MI6 in October 1951. Follwing three years of probationary service—and glowing reports—Hedley had been posted to Budapest as an Associated Press correspondent. There was only one flaw in Hedley's otherwise impeccable record.

The man who had recommended his acceptance was Kim Philby.

"Four days, that's all you spent in custody." Deakin allowed himself another bleak smile. "Friend Khrushchev was pretty quick off the mark, wasn't he?"

"He needed to be," Hedley said in a level voice. "One provocative move by the government now could spark off a revolution."

"Come now, don't you think you're exaggerating the situation?"

"Does the name Lazlo Rajk mean anything to you?"

"I've done my share of background reading," Deakin said caustically. "He was the Minister of Home Affairs in the first postwar government."

"Then you'll also recall that when Tito broke with Stalin in 1949, the Kremlin ordered the Hungarian government to stage a show trial to prove to fellow Communists that Tito was behind an anti-Soviet conspiracy. The Prime Minister of the day chose Rajk simply because he was a dangerous rival, and in due

7

course Rajk was tried, condemned, and executed. Right?"

Deakin nodded and glanced at his wristwatch. It was just past 9:30; he recalled the instructions he'd received from Charles Pelham Winter: "Give me a progress report as soon as you can, George. Eden will have heard about Hedley's deportation by now and I must have some answers when I see Bracecourt at the Foreign Office tomorrow morning. Geraldine's giving one of her famous dinner parties tonight, but don't let that stop you. I'll be glad of an excuse to slip away."

"So what about Rajk?" Deakin said.

"This coming Saturday, Rajk will be reburied in the main cemetery of Budapest. Saturday, the sixth of October, *also* happens to be the anniversary of the 1869 Hungarian War of Independence against Austria."

The Hungarian War of Independence. Deakin frowned and closed his eyes; he could imagine Winter's reaction to that particular piece of information, could hear too the faintly condescending tone of voice that rarely failed to touch a raw nerve. Winter was always condescending. From the moment of his birth, life had been one long primrose path: Eton, Magdalen College, Oxford, the Brigade of Guards, then, in 1938, at the age of twenty-six, marriage to the Honorable Geraldine Montague. With his social connections, Winter was predestined to reach the top of the ladder. That he should also possess a good brain seemed doubly unfair to Deakin. He resented everything Winter stood for.

Hedley said, "If there are a lot of question marks against my name, you can rub them out seventy-two hours from now. The Hungarian uprising starts on Saturday when 150,000 people march through the streets of Budapest as a mark of respect for Lazlo Rajk."

At last, Deakin thought, *he's told me something that can be corroborated, something that will get me off the hook with Winter.*

"That should bring the traffic to a grinding halt, if nothing else." Deakin glanced at his wristwatch again. "I think it's time we called a halt," he said. "You've had more than enough

8

for one day. I don't know about you, but I'm feeling a bit peckish. Fancy a ham sandwich or something?"

"No thanks," said Hedley. "I ate on the plane. All I want to do now is crawl into bed."

"I'll get the valet to show you to your room." Deakin smiled. "I think you'll find we've provided everything necessary."

Deakin was just a shade too eager to be rid of him now. Hedley guessed he would be on the telephone the moment he was safely out of earshot. He wondered what Deakin would say.

2.

Winter decided that Jeffrey Vallance was easily the most obnoxious individual it had ever been his misfortune to meet. He was the kind of author who, though unsuccessful, believed in dressing the part. All the male guests were in dinner jackets except for Vallance. He was wearing a pink shirt and a floppy bow tie with a velvet smoking jacket and gabardine slacks that looked as if they had been pressed under a mattress. His style of dress was, however, the least objectionable thing about him. It was his massive conceit and hectoring manner that really put Winter's back up.

He also cursed the editor of whatever crummy little magazine it was who had commissioned Vallance to do a series of articles on the Middle East crisis. Having just returned from Cyprus where he'd spent two weeks annoying every public relations officer on the staff of General Keightley's headquarters, Vallance was now determined to give him the benefit of his wisdom.

"The whole idea of using Cyprus as a base for the invasion of Egypt is simply preposterous." Vallance swallowed the last of his gin and held out the glass for a refill. "There's no deep water harbor, the only airfield of any consequence is Nicosia, and most of the garrison is tied down fighting the EOKA terrorists."

"I don't see any alternative," Winter said mildly. "It's the only base we have in the eastern Mediterranean."

Vallance had him pinned in the corner by the drinks wagon, blocking the only avenue of escape. In mounting desperation, he glanced across the room, hoping somebody would leave the roulette table and come to his rescue, but all he got was a sympathetic smile from Katherine Lang. Winter didn't blame her for ignoring his mute appeal for help; Vallance was a last minute substitute for Katherine's husband who'd had to take off for New York on business, and she'd had to suffer him all through dinner.

"Well, I agree Malta is even worse than useless, but that's my whole point, Winter."

"What point?"

"The fact that the army is planning to use a sledgehammer to crack a nut. My God, the way they're carrying on you'd think the Huns were sitting on the Canal."

Winter sighed. The evening had got off to a bad start when he'd arrived home late from the office, leaving himself just ten minutes in which to shower and change for dinner before their guests arrived. It had then got progressively worse from the moment he'd informed Geraldine that he was expecting a telephone call from George Deakin and might well have to slip away before any of their guests departed. Many wives confronted with a similar situation would probably have made a scene, but not Geraldine; she had infinitely more subtle ways of conveying her displeasure. Instead of angry words and accusations, she had simply rearranged the seating plan, removing Katherine Lang from his right in order to saddle him with two boring companions instead of one. A telling move that, because Katherine was a vivacious brunette and one of their friends of whom he was more than just a little fond. Minus husband, he found her doubly attractive.

"As I was saying to Garnett before we went in to dinner . . ."

"Who?"

"Garnett." Vallance pointed his glass toward a slim man in horn-rimmed spectacles who had volunteered to be the croupier. "The Parliamentary Private Secretary."

"His name is Garner," Winter said bleakly.

"Oh really?" Vallance shrugged his shoulders. "I can't imagine how I could have forgotten so soon, especially after the way his wife kept on about his great political future. To hear her talk, you'd think he'd already got a foot inside the door of Number 10."

"There's nothing wrong with being ambitious," Winter said, as if that explained everything.

Vallance grunted and stared at his still empty glass. "Where was I?" he demanded.

"I think you were about to give me your views on what is wrong with our military strategy." Winter took the empty glass from Vallance and fixed him another gin and tonic.

Once started on the subject of military strategy, there was no holding Vallance. Facts, figures, grandiose tactical plans for retaking the Canal were delivered in a seemingly endless monologue. Bored beyond endurance, Winter let it all go in through one ear and out the other while nodding sagely at appropriate intervals, as though deeply interested in what Vallance had to say.

"Not that I approve of Eden's policy, old man."

"You don't?"

"Good God, no! The man's taken leave of his senses. I mean, if the Suez Canal is so damned vital, why did he agree to withdraw our troops back in 1954 when he was Secretary of State for Foreign Affairs? Answer me that if you can."

Winter declined to accept the challenge. For one thing, explaining to Vallance just how and why this had come about would be a waste of breath. For another, good old George Deakin had finally come to his rescue.

"Excuse me," he said. "I'll be back in a minute."

"What?"

"The telephone's ringing," said Winter. "Can't you hear it?"

Vallance shook his head. "I must be getting deaf in my old age."

"It happens to us all sooner or later," Winter said, and slipped out of the room.

Closing the door behind him, he walked across the hall and entered his study where he could talk to Deakin in peace and quiet.

Deakin said, "I haven't telephoned at an inopportune moment, have I?"

"You couldn't have chosen a better time," Winter assured him.

"Good. Only you did say you wanted a progress report."

"I did indeed." Winter sat down and propped his feet up on the desk. "What did you make of Hedley's story, George?"

"It's too early yet to say whether he's on the level, Charles."

"I was referring to the manifesto the Mikes are supposed to have shown him in Budapest."

"You know about that?"

"A cable arrived from Vienna after you'd left the office. According to our people who met him at the frontier, Hedley was suffering from a bad case of verbal diarrhea. Seems he didn't stop chattering until they put him on the plane for Heathrow."

"Well, in that case, there's nothing more to be said, is there?"

"I disagree," Winter said quickly. "We've got to do something about Hedley. I think you and I should put our heads together."

"All in good time, Charles. There's a long way to go yet."

Deakin was coldly polite, but the message was clear enough. Hedley was his concern and he should back off and leave well enough alone.

"Listen, George," Winter said urgently, "there are problems we have to talk about, problems that can't be discussed over the telephone." A burst of laughter reached him from across the hall and glancing around, he saw Katherine Lang standing in the doorway, a faint mocking smile on her lips. "I can be with you in thirty minutes," he continued in a low voice.

"You're coming over here tonight?" Deakin sounded incredulous.

"Is there any reason why I shouldn't?"

"Look," said Deakin, "I don't want to appear rude, but it's been a long day and I'm tired."

"You and me both," Winter said and put down the phone.

"You're a sly one, Charles." Katherine moved inside the study and closed the door behind her. "Running out on your own party?"

"You know how it is—duty calls and all that sort of thing." Winter swung his feet off the desk and stood up. "Anyway, what's your excuse for beating a retreat?"

"I'm afraid the stakes were becoming a little too high for me, Charles."

"Who's losing the most?"

"Give you one guess."

"Geraldine?"

"She's certainly playing with reckless abandon."

"Well, that's Geraldine for you," he said, moving several paces nearer Katherine. "She always did have this cavalier attitude toward money."

The large Edwardian house facing Hampstead Heath and all it contained except the silver was hers. The social position she owed to her grandfather, a prosperous mill owner who had been knighted for political services to the Liberal Party before the turn of the century. From rags to riches to rags again in three generations: it happened often enough, and it was happening here—both father and daughter seemed hell-bent on dissipating their inheritance.

"I'm sorry this evening has been such a bore," he said.

"I assume you're referring to Jeffrey Vallance?" Katherine laughed and shook her head. "What an insufferable little man he is."

"You have me to thank for that." Winter reached out and entwined his fingers in hers.

"You?"

"I arrived home late, so to get her own back, Geraldine rearranged the seating plan. That's how you were stuck with Vallance."

"They do say revenge is sweet," she murmured.

"You win a few, lose a few." Winter cleared his throat. "How long is Harry staying in New York?"

"He hopes to be home by the weekend."

"That soon?"

"I'm still a grass widow until Saturday morning," she said meaningfully.

They were standing very close now, their knees almost touching, and he couldn't remember when Katherine had been quite so desirable. The green velvet dress helped of course; it showed off her figure, emphasizing every subtle curve.

"Pity about tonight," he said in a husky voice. "I could have offered to run you home."

"You could always stop off at my place for a nightcap on your way back."

"That's an idea." Her mouth looked very inviting, the lips moist and apart. "But I don't know how long I'll be gone. It could be until the early hours of the morning."

"Try not to wake the neighbors then," she said and kissed him lightly. "Now I'd better go before the others miss me."

Winter nodded. Always discreet, always careful; you could say that was their motto, the reason why Harry and Geraldine had never suspected they were lovers. He wondered how Katherine would explain her absence from the party, but then the toilet flushed in the downstairs cloakroom and his unspoken question was answered. Leaving the study, Winter collected an overcoat and scarf from the rack in the hall and quietly let himself out of the house.

Deakin threw another log on the fire and sank back in the armchair. He didn't see how Winter could drive all the way out to Burnham House from Hampstead Heath in half an hour, but of course there wouldn't be much traffic on the roads at this time of night and he did own a Jaguar. The car, like the large Edwardian house on Spaniards Road, was a sign of affluence and a visible reminder that he and Charles lived in two different worlds. This had been very evident on the one and only occasion the Winters had entertained the Deakins. Lunchtime drinks on a Sunday instead of dinner at eight, because they were numbered amongst the lesser fry. He had wanted to plead a previous engagement, but Marjorie had pleaded with him to accept and had been tremendously impressed with everything she saw, especially the silver and the Meissen ornaments displayed in nook cabinets. So very different from their little three-bedroom, semidetached house in Hendon.

Their house? Not when it had been bought and paid for by Marjorie's first husband, not when his stepdaughter Coral made him feel like an interloper. She had always resented him, right from the moment he began to take an interest in her mother. They had met in Zermatt in January 1951, two lonely adults on a package skiing holiday. The restaurant had been crowded that first night and he could still remember the sulky expression on Coral's face when, in desperation, the head waiter had showed him to their table. Six months later they were married, the confirmed bachelor home from the Middle East and the widow of a schoolmaster with a sixteen-year-old daughter.

Deakin heard the crunch of tire on gravel as a car came up the drive and immediately glanced at the clock on the mantelpiece. Forty minutes from door to door was not bad going, but by his own reckoning, Charles was ten minutes late. Somehow he found that oddly reassuring.

The Jaguar pulled up near the front porch and there was a loud clunk as Winter got out of the car and slammed the door behind him. Deakin half rose from his chair, suddenly realized that the porter at the lodge would have buzzed the house to warn the staff to expect him, and promptly sat down again. Moments later, Winter breezed into the library, looking distinguished and debonair in a dark overcoat and white silk scarf.

"Sorry I'm late, George." Winter removed his coat and scarf and made straight for the drinks tray, helping himself to a whiskey and soda. "I'm afraid the journey took longer than I'd anticipated."

"A lot of traffic?" Deakin asked.

"No. It was the lights; they seemed to be against me all the way."

"Hard luck."

"Yes, wasn't it." Winter sat down in a chair facing him. "Now," he said abruptly, "what about Hedley?"

"Well, Charles, as I've already said, it's early days yet."

"Quite so. However, we are in a position to draw at least one conclusion. Whether he's red or blue, we can never use Hedley in the field again. His face will be too well-known. Right?"

"Agreed."

"And in view of his comparative lack of experience, we can't find him a suitable desk job, can we?"

"So what are we going to do with him?" said Deakin. "Put him out to grass?"

"The opposition would certainly expect us to regard him with suspicion, and maybe we should. But double agents do have their uses."

Deakin stared into the fire. Winter had drifted into the Intelligence world shortly after his battalion was evacuated from Dunkirk. His qualifications had been practically nil but in those days influence still counted for a lot, and the fact that he had covered the Spanish civil war as a free-lance journalist probably tipped the scales in his favor. It was, after all, an era when the swashbuckler was in vogue. Still, whatever the reason for his ultimate selection, he had certainly made his name in counter-espionage. Those who had known him during the war years still recalled the brilliant way he had turned captured agents and used them to send bogus information to the Abwehr. Apparently he now had much the same plans for Hedley.

"Head-hunting?" Deakin said, voicing his thoughts aloud. "Shouldn't we leave that to MI5?"

"I'm not sure I'm with you, George."

"I thought you were hinting that we might use Hedley as bait to catch a few sprats."

"We seem to be talking at cross purposes." Winter smiled. "I had a much more devious plan in mind."

"Such as?"

"Well, George, in the little matter of the Suez Canal, you tell me who is being the most difficult—Nasser or Dulles?"

It was a question which should properly have been asked of Bill Turnock, Deakin's erstwhile assistant, who had taken over the running of the Mideast desk since early June. Deakin knew Winter didn't think much of Turnock, though. On matters affecting the Middle East, it was still Deakin he turned to.

"Dulles," Deakin said emphatically.

"Exactly. The Maritime Nations Conference, the Suez Canal Users Association—you name it, Dulles has used every device he can to prevent us from taking action against Nasser. Now, what if we were to give him something else to worry about? Like Hungary, for instance."

"I think you've just lost me," said Deakin.

"Suppose we allowed Hedley to tell his story to the Americans?"

Deakin produced a pipe from his jacket pocket and began to fill it from a leather pouch. "It could be a way of getting Dulles off our backs," he said thoughtfully.

"And point our friends in the right direction. Who controls the bloody Canal is only part of our quarrel with Nasser. It's really about oil, George, and the long-term threat to our economy. Unless that tinpot dictator is cut down to size and we achieve some sort of stability in the Middle East, our precious oil supplies are always going to be in jeopardy."

"You're beginning to sound like Eden," Deakin said in a mild tone of reproof.

"So what? He happens to be right." Winter stared at him over the rim of his glass. "The PM made it very clear to Khrushchev and Bulganin when they were over here in April that, if necessary, we would fight to secure our oil supplies. It's possible they thought he was bluffing; that's why we need the Americans with their big stick. We need them to control the Russian Bear if it starts growling."

"And after Hedley has spoken to our transatlantic friends?"

"We'll keep him here for a day or two and then turn him loose. Naturally, we'll put a tail on him."

"Naturally." Deakin struck a match and held it over the bowl of his pipe. "I take it that as Head of Administration you will be making all the necessary arrangements?"

"Of course." Winter finished his whiskey and stood up. "You've warned your wife you're staying the night here, have you, George?" he said disarmingly.

"No, I haven't. I was hoping you were going to offer me a lift back to town."

"Can't be done, I'm afraid. You see, Tom McNulty will be arriving here at ten o'clock tomorrow morning."

"McNulty?" Deakin blinked his eyes. "Who's he?"

"The top CIA man in London," Winter said coolly.

3.

The black Cadillac was almost as wide as the gravel driveway and nearly twice the length of the average British car. Watching the limousine as it moved off toward the lodge, Hedley thought the large American sedan with its diplomatic plates looked wholly out of place in the rural surroundings of Burnham House.

"I wonder they didn't fly the Stars and Stripes while they were at it," Deakin observed acidly. "After all, it's possible some of the villagers may not have noticed them."

"One did get the impression they were anxious to draw attention to themselves," Hedley said dryly.

"Determined would be more accurate." Deakin moved away from the window and retrieved the small envelope lying on the coffee table which McNulty had given him by way of a parting gift. "Miles Abbott should have had more sense than to allow them to arrive here in that damned great bus."

"Miles Abbott? Was he the character sitting up front with the chauffeur?"

"That's him."

"Obviously ex-Army," said Hedley. "I bet he works for 'The Firm.'"

Deakin nodded. "In Admin. Winter telephoned while you

were having breakfast to say that he'd arranged for one of his people to meet McNulty at the embassy. Abbott should have insisted they use his car. This is supposed to be a safe house, but now everyone around here knows about it."

Hedley doubted if they did, but Deakin's ill humor was understandable. The briefing session on the Hungarian political scene had gone down like a lead balloon.

"What did you make of Janet Roscoe?" he asked.

"I thought she was a pretty little thing," Deakin said without looking up from the snapshots he was studying.

Hedley smiled. McNulty had brought along a colleague from the State Department and the description was both misleading and inaccurate. The American girl was hardly little; she was about 5'7" in her low-heeled shoes, and pretty was usually the kind of adjective most people attached to a face that was instantly forgettable. Janet Roscoe was different; her face would stand out in a crowd and be remembered for the high cheekbones, the widely spaced and deep-set eyes, the generous mouth, and the firm jaw. Her hair was a shiny brown, the color of a horse chestnut, and the waves had looked natural. Although no great expert when it came to guessing a woman's age, he thought she was probably somewhere in her late twenties.

"She's quite intelligent too," Deakin added in an abrupt afterthought.

"Yes," Hedley said. "Even had me pinned in a corner a couple of times."

"So I noticed. Somehow I don't believe Miss Roscoe was altogether impressed with your story. Come to that, neither was McNulty." Deakin passed the snapshots to Hedley with a wry smile. "You can tell from these what he thinks of the SIS."

The photographs, three in number, showed a short, stockily built, middle-aged Russian in naval uniform, the fur earflaps of his *shapkamikovya* tied above the crown. In two of the exposures, the subject was posed on the bridge of a fast patrol boat while the third had been taken outside the headquarters of the Soviet Baltic Fleet.

"His face looks vaguely familiar," Hedley said presently.

"McNulty claims it is none other than Commander Lionel 'Buster' Crabb." *Crabb*, thought Deakin. *Now there was a name and a botched operation the SIS would like to forget.* A highly decorated frogman who'd left the Royal Navy some years ago, Crabb had been dug out of retirement by a control officer and taken down to Portsmouth to examine the hull of the *Ordzhonkidze*, the Sverdlov Class cruiser which Khrushchev and Bulganin had used when they had visited England back in April. The operation had been a minidisaster. It hadn't been cleared with the Foreign Office, and Crabb, who was a near alcoholic with a fetish for going to bed in a rubber wet suit, had been poisoned by the buildup of carbon dioxide in his oxygen rebreathing apparatus. The body had been swept out to sea, but not before the Russians had found out about it. Khrushchev had thought it a huge joke and it had made them the laughingstock of the world—except that, like Queen Victoria, Eden had not been amused.

"Is there any chance these snapshots could be genuine?" asked Hedley.

"Not in a million years," said Deakin. "Crabb is dead and McNulty knows it. He's just having a little fun at our expense."

"He has an unpleasant sense of humor."

Deakin smiled. So did Winter, and it was a stone cold certainty that McNulty wouldn't be laughing by the time he had finished with him.

Winter heard the telephone ringing in his office as he stepped out of the lift and began to saunter along the corridor. Its shrill summons irritated him and at first he was tempted to ignore it, but a sudden hunch that the caller was probably George Deakin prompted him to quicken his stride. Entering the office, he shucked off his raincoat and, draping it on the hatstand, he hurried over to the desk to answer the phone.

In an aggrieved voice, Deakin said, "Is that you, Charles?"

"It is." Winter moved around the desk and in the process stubbed his foot against the black oblong-shaped box on the floor. "Sod it," he said furiously, "if that isn't the last bloody straw."

"What is?" Deakin inquired.

"The scrambler, George. I've just tripped over the damned thing."

"I hope you haven't damaged anything, Charles."

Deakin seemed concerned but he wasn't sure whether George was referring to him or the scrambler.

"I don't think any bones are broken," he said. "I'm not sure about the scrambler, but we'll know soon enough. Are you ready to switch to secure?"

"Yes."

"Good." Winter depressed a button on the telephone and a small green bulb below the cradle lit up. Glancing down, he saw that a light was showing on the panel of the black box. "Everything appears to be in order this end," he said.

"That's a relief." Deakin cleared his throat. "Your American friends left over twenty minutes ago and I've been trying to reach you ever since. Where have you been?"

Deakin was beginning to sound like Geraldine. There was the same plaintive whine to his voice and only a few short hours ago she too had asked him where he'd been when he'd crept into her bed fresh from Katherine's.

"The Foreign Office," he snapped. "Where else?"

"Yes, of course. I'm afraid I'd completely forgotten you had to brief them this morning. How did they take the news?"

Winter sighed. "To tell you the truth, George, it didn't arouse much interest. As a matter of fact, Bracecourt kept me waiting a good two hours. He's much more concerned with the meeting Selwyn Lloyd and Christian Pineau, the French Foreign Minister, are due to have with Dulles tomorrow. As if it made any difference. Dulles and Eisenhower are determined to stay in our hair—meeting's a damn waste of time."

"It would seem we've both had an unproductive morning then," said Deakin. "Hedley did his best, but he failed to get the message across. So far as the CIA and the State Department are concerned, the Suez Canal is still the major flashpoint."

"Never mind, George, it was worth a try."

Obviously it would take more than an unconfirmed report from a discredited agent to impress Tom McNulty. Well, perhaps it could be arranged.

"There's something else you should know, Charles. By way of a parting gift, McNulty gave me three snapshots of Commander Crabb which are alleged to have been taken in Kronshtadt."

"That's impossible. He's dead."

"Or so we'd like to believe," said Deakin. "Unfortunately, in the absence of a body, there's no conclusive proof that he was drowned at sea, is there?"

"One would think the CIA were determined to embarrass us in any way they can, George."

"You could be right. In the meantime, what are we going to do about these snapshots?"

Winter thought a moment. Yes. "They're undoubtedly a red herring, but we'll go through the motions, take a fresh look at the evidence. That's a job Hedley can do."

"Hedley?" Deakin's voice rose in disbelief. "But we haven't cleared him yet."

"What are you worried about, George? Hedley is no longer your responsibility; I'm taking him off your hands."

"When?"

"This afternoon, just as soon as you can deliver him to 22 Gresham Square."

"All right," said Deakin, his voice still puzzled. "I'll have him there by three o'clock."

Winter put the phone down and glanced at his wristwatch. Miles Abbott should be back in the office before one o'clock which would give him at least two hours to find the relevant file on Commander Crabb and get himself around to the safe house in Gresham Square. Hedley would be short of money, but he had a month's salary coming to him and Abbott could take care of that too, drawing the necessary cash from the Imprest Account. Naval Intelligence would have to be consulted if they were going to provide a suitable expert to keep Hedley on the

24

right lines, and no doubt that would take a certain amount of time.

So how about Monday? Winter nodded. Yes, he would send Hedley down to Portsmouth on Monday and, at the same time, remove the ground from under Tom McNulty's feet before he got to hear about it and started crowing. Keeping Hedley occupied while Abbott did the spadework on the other operation was the only reason to reopen the Crabb investigation; and it would do no harm to hint as much to McNulty. The American's reaction to the Hungarian situation had been a disappointment, but Winter had a simple rule: when you were repulsed on one front, you launched a counterattack on another.

1956

Monday, October 8 to Thursday, October 25

4.

The staff canteen provided a bottomless pit of raw material for the wags of 54 Broadway. The food was invariably lukewarm and unappetizing, the hot plate was forever breaking down, the central heating system only functioned in fits and starts, and the decor reflected the prevailing mania of the Ministry of Public Works and Buildings for dark green paint. With the exception of George Deakin and Bill Turnock, senior officers never ate there if they could possibly help it. Deakin, who was anything but a gourmet, patronized the canteen because it was convenient and very cheap. Turnock, who liked to think he possessed a more educated palate, did so because he had got into the habit of lunching with Deakin while serving as his assistant, a practice he found hard to break despite the fact that they no longer worked in the same section.

"There's one thing to be said in favor of this place," Turnock observed lugubriously.

Deakin eyed the piece of sausage speared on his fork. "Oh yes? What's that?"

"You can talk shop without breaking the rules."

"Are you about to tell me something, Bill?"

Turnock shook his head. "I wanted to ask you about Hedley.

Is it true that Winter has taken him under his wing?"

"He's arranged for him to be attached to Admin."

"Before he was cleared, George?"

"Charles may have jumped the lights, but they turned to green after Lazlo Rajk's funeral on Saturday."

Turncock swallowed a last mouthful of mashed potato, placed his knife and fork together, and wiped his lips on a paper napkin. "I still don't like it," he grumbled. "Something very fishy is going on."

"I can't see why you're worried," Deakin said mildly. "After all, Hedley is not your responsibility."

"Maybe so, but I'm not happy about the way Winter keeps prying into my affairs. He's not running the Arabian desk, but only this morning he dropped into my office to suggest that I should establish a much closer liaison with my opposite number in France. I told him what he could do with his idea."

Deakin pushed his plate aside and brought out his pipe. It was very doubtful if Turnock had done anything of the kind. He had only just been promoted and was still unsure of himself.

"What did Charles say to that?" he asked.

"Nothing, but three-quarters of an hour later I received a summons from Deputy Control who calmly informed me that I was booked on the 9:05 BEA flight to Paris tomorrow. I got the strong impression that Winter had put him up to it."

Deakin thought that was more than likely. As a direct result of Kim Philby's suspension, coupled with the backlash from the Crabb affair, the SIS was now in the process of being reorganized from top to bottom, and rumor had it that Winter was slated to be the next Deputy Control. If that was true, Charles was merely anticipating events by a few weeks, perhaps even days.

"He also said it would give me an opportunity to meet old adversaries from faraway places, which I didn't think was very funny, George."

He sounded bitter, and Deakin knew the reason. Hedley was not the only man familiar with Tel Aviv. Turnock was a former Colonial policeman who had spent the greater part of his service in Palestine. Because he was one of the best officers in Special Branch, the Irgun Zvai Leumi had put a price of £2,000 on his head and he'd had to leave the country in a hurry.

"You're meeting the Israelis, aren't you, Bill?" he said quietly.

Turnock nodded. "Two high-ranking Intelligence officers from their Mossad Department; Control didn't tell me their names. Wouldn't it be a laugh if one of them turned out to be Esther Rabinowitz?"

The high school teacher, the twenty-two-year-old girl with raven-black hair who had lived with Turnock and then betrayed him to the Irgun Zvai Leumi. Deakin recalled there had been a note to that effect in his personal file, a sort of black mark that could spell trouble for him in the future. The Foreign Office was pro-Arab but should there be a change of attitude, Bill could find himself out of a job. People would start to say that Turnock should have known better. Deakin had seen a snapshot of him in khaki drill and even in those far-off days he'd been no oil painting. His thighs had been decidedly flabby, there was the beginning of a double chin, and his sandy hair had been very thin on top. Add a pair of narrow eyes and a straggly mustache and it was hard to believe that an attractive young woman could possibly have been interested in him.

"We must be mad, George. If we ally ourselves with Israel, we'll have the whole Arab world against us."

"Tell that to Winter," said Deakin. "He seems to be running the show these days."

McNulty opened the communicating door between the two offices and sauntered into the adjoining room where Janet Roscoe had installed herself when she was seconded to him from Langley, Virginia, displacing his secretary who had reluctantly moved out into the typing pool. The small typing desk had been exchanged for one that had two sets of drawers and an executive model with padded armrests had replaced the swivel chair, but so far she had made no attempt to rearrange the furniture.

The desk was where it had always been, diagonally across the far corner of the room near the window overlooking Grosvenor Square.

"Hi," he said. "I'm back. Any messages for me?"

Janet looked up. "The telephone hasn't rung all afternoon."

"Cables?"

"Nothing from Langley," she said, "but there was one from the Ambassador to Washington which was passed to us for information. Someone in Eden's cabinet is keeping Ambassador Aldrich extremely well-informed. Do you want to see it?"

"Not particularly." McNulty moved to the window and stood there gazing down on Grosvenor Square, hands in pockets. "I have my own sources," he said.

"Do I gather you had a successful lunch?"

"Yeah. Winter was in great form." McNulty pressed his forehead against the cool windowpane. Lunch at Claridge's with Charles Winter had been altogether too successful. They had consumed the best part of two bottles of Morey-Saint-Denis and the splitting headache was a reminder that he should never have had that large brandy with his coffee.

"Do you have any aspirins?" he asked.

"In my handbag. I'll fetch you a glass of ice water to wash them down. Or would you prefer a cup of black coffee?"

"Ice water will do me fine, Jan."

McNulty closed his eyes and tried to ignore the gurgle from the water cooler as she filled a paper cup for him. In another hour he could call it a day and go home, but the next sixty minutes were going to seem like purgatory.

"Two aspirins and ice water coming up." Janet dropped the tablets into the palm of his outstretched hand and smiled sympathetically. "You sure look off-color, Tom."

"I feel like I look." McNulty popped the tablets into his mouth and swilled them down. "Thanks," he said, returning the cup. "Now maybe I can get through what's left of the afternoon."

"Why bother to try? Your in tray is empty and I can't see

anything cropping up between now and five o'clock that I can't handle."

How little you know, McNulty thought. Aloud he said, "Tell me, what did you make of James Hedley?"

"I'm not sure." Janet reached into her handbag, took out a packet of Chesterfields, and lit a cigarette. "At first I thought his story was just a little *too* plausible, but it's certainly gained in credibility after what happened in Budapest on Saturday. He's obviously intelligent and quick-witted, but . . . treading warily, I would say. He didn't give much away."

"Would it surprise you to know that he's no longer in quarantine?"

"After Burgess and Maclean, nothing the SIS did could surprise me."

"Don't write them off as a busted flush, Jan. Hungary is one ball game where they're way ahead of us."

It was a fluke of course, but Winter was certainly making the most of it, positively rubbing his hands with glee. Nevertheless, Hedley's information was too strong to be dismissed out of hand. Like it or not, Washington simply couldn't afford to ignore it. . . .

"What about those Crabb snapshots?" Janet asked.

McNulty turned about and perched himself on the edge of the windowsill. "Didn't believe them for a minute. Just shrugged them off. Damn, I thought we could take a little wind out of his sails there."

"And now it's boomeranged on you."

McNulty thought he detected a note of criticism, but he let it pass. "In fact, Winter was just a shade too confident. Which leads me to think he may have another ace up his sleeve."

"Oh yes?"

"He's taken Hedley under his wing, moved him into a flat in Gresham Square." McNulty cleared his throat. "I think you'd better make a note of his address."

"Why?" Janet asked. Her voice was ice-cold, as if she already knew the answer.

"Because I think he could be Winter's errand boy and I want you to get close to him." Anger showed in her green eyes and he didn't like the set of her jaw. "Don't get me wrong," McNulty added hastily. "It's a routine job."

"I think I ought to make one thing crystal clear," she said angrily. "I'm not going to get laid for you or anyone else."

"Nobody's asking you to."

"That's all right then." Janet picked up a pencil. "What did you say the address was?"

"22 Gresham Square. I've looked it up on the map and it's a cul-de-sac off Kensington High Street." He could tell Janet was still mad by the way she pressed down on the pencil. "I want you to set up a surveillance mission. Think you can handle it?"

"I know I can," Janet said quietly. "When do we start?"

"As soon as possible. I don't know why Winter was so keen for me to know that Hedley had moved into Gresham Square, but time will tell. He tried to give the impression that it was a slip of the tongue, but I'm betting it was deliberate." McNulty pinched the lobe of his right ear, an unconscious habit when deep in thought. "We'll need to put some of our best people on this," he said. "That being the case, you'd better call on Kaplin. He runs a good team."

"Thanks, Tom." Janet consulted her brief notes and frowned. "Obviously we'll have to look the place over and find a stake-out," she said, voicing her thoughts aloud. "Until we can come up with a more permanent arrangement, we'll simply cover the High Street with a few pedestrians. They could be in place early tomorrow morning."

"Good." McNulty stood up and moved toward the communicating door. "Just keep me informed, okay?"

"I guess that means you'll be calling all the shots?"

"You can bet on that," said McNulty.

The pubs had closed long ago, the buses were no longer running, and although their semidetached on Queen's Road was some distance from the station, Deakin fancied he could hear

34

the last down train to Edgware approaching Hendon Central. Soon there would be utter peace and quiet and then maybe he would finally drop off to sleep. With Marjorie grinding her teeth beside him? While he could see the orange glare of a streetlight through a chink in the curtains? When his brain was too active? He could plug his ears and shut his eyes but there was nothing he could do about his mind.

The images flashed through his brain like a montage of film clips. The first Friday in March when they learned that King Hussein had sacked Lieutenant General Sir John Glubb, giving the commander of his Arab Legion just twelve hours to get out of Jordan, and wrecking the Baghdad Pact. Nasser had broken the news to Selwyn Lloyd while the Foreign Secretary was taking his leave of him and no one had doubted that Glubb's dismissal, the riots in the street, the destruction of the pact, had been instigated by Cairo Radio. Winter had been in a fine rage all day, his hatred evenly divided between Nasser and Dulles.

Another Friday: this time the fourth of May and the aftermath of the Crabb affair. For over a fortnight they had been waiting for the balloon to go up and the tension had been so unbearable that the final explosion had come almost as a relief. Except for some who remembered it as the day of the Inquisition and the block. More than a few heads had rolled that afternoon, and suddenly he'd found himself in charge of the Russian desk.

The images followed one another with bewildering speed. The nationalization of the Suez Canal, the mobilization of the Army Emergency Reserve, and the detailed planning of the invasion of Egypt, an operation that had originally been known as Hamilcar before it had become Musketeer on the whim of a corps commander who was a fan of Dumas. And now there was Hungary, and Winter using every means at his disposal to drive a wedge between Eisenhower and Dulles. And Bill Turnock leaving for Paris in a few hours time to have secret talks with the Israelis. Was this the road that led from Sarajevo, then?

Deakin opened his eyes again, stared at the orange glare between the curtains, and saw a fireball many times brighter than the sun. "There's going to be a major war," he said aloud and felt his blood run cold.

5.

They sat in a row facing Winter: Turnock on the left, Deakin in the center, and Miles Abbott on the right nursing a couple of manila folders on his lap. Almost two hours had elapsed since Winter had summoned them to his office for a round table conference at eleven o'clock, and Turnock was still in the hot seat. On reflection, Deakin came to the conclusion that perhaps witness box would be a more apt description in view of the way Bill was being cross-examined about his liaison visit to Paris.

A *sign of the times,* he mused. Winter might still be using the same office, but he'd moved up the ladder to Deputy Control and was evidently determined to make an impression in his new post. That he should want to know everything Bill had learned from the French and Israeli Intelligence officers was only natural, but it was hard to shake off the impression that this debriefing session had been arranged largely for the benefit of George Deakin. It was as if Charles was determined to open his eyes to the facts of life, to prove beyond all reasonable doubt that an armed clash in the Middle East was inevitable.

But if such was the case, why had Miles Abbott been invited to attend? Miles was an errand boy for Administration, not a

Section head. A sudden thought occurred to Deakin and he almost bit through the stem of his pipe. Incredible as it might seem, could it be that Abbott was due to take over as Head of Administration from Winter? The question proved obsessive and he found himself listening to Turnock with only half an ear.

"The French were quite open with me," Turnock said, drawing to a conclusion. "They made no secret of the fact that they have already delivered a significant number of AMX 13 tanks to Israel. They've also dipped into their NATO stocks—trucks, self-propelled guns, ammunition—you name it, they're shipping it out."

Winter smiled. "Without the knowledge of SAC Europe, Bill?" he asked slyly.

"Much of the equipment is American, so naturally they want to keep it from General Gruenther."

"That's all very commendable, but I doubt if it has been possible to achieve a complete blackout."

Turnock pinched his eyes. He felt tired and his throat was sore. The weariness was understandable; contrary to what he'd been led to believe, the talks in Paris had lasted a full two days and he'd come straight to the office from the airport. Rather than a strained voice, the sore throat was more likely to be the beginning of a foul cold, which would explain why he found it difficult to concentrate.

"Are you referring to the Mystères or the conversion course the French are running for the Israelis?"

"Both," said Winter.

"The conversion course is very hush-hush. The pilots are keeping a low profile and uniforms are taboo because they are using a civilian airfield somewhere in the back of beyond. With any luck, the Israelis will be back in their own country before the Americans get wind of their presence. The Mystères are a different matter. The air staff at SHAPE are aware that three squadrons have been moved south but current thinking is that the French intend to use them in Algeria without reference to SACEUR. In fact, they're already in Tel Aviv along with a whole load of French instructors who are busy teaching the Israeli ground staff how to service them. No specific date was mentioned but if you want an educated guess, I'd say those three fighter squadrons will be fully operational by the twenty-first of October, ten days from now."

"Ten days from now," Winter repeated in a soft voice, and then added sharply, "What do you make of it all, George?"

Deakin stared at the pattern of raindrops on the window and wondered how best to answer the question without offending Bill Turnock. Another question which should have been directed to Bill.

"The French pride themselves on being realistic," he said presently. "They're not impressed by our military preparations because they believe we'll suddenly develop cold feet when it really comes to the crunch. The Israelis are different again; they've had itchy feet ever since we pulled out of the Canal Zone and the British Army ceased to be an effective buffer between them and the Egyptians. Our withdrawal left the way clear for Nasser to reinforce his army in the Sinai and it encouraged the Fedayeen commandos to step up their attacks against Jewish settlements. The Israelis thought they could contain the guerrilla menace by launching a series of cross border raids on the Fedayeen bases, but they changed their ideas when Nasser announced his arms deal with the Czechs. From then on, it was only a question of time before they embarked on a preemptive war against Egypt." Deakin broke off and glanced at Turnock. "At least that is the conclusion Bill and I reached when we learned the Soviets were using the back door to pour arms into Egypt."

Winter was quite sure that Deakin was giving credit where none was due, but that was typical of George. Turnock was his protégé and, recognizing his inadequacies, he never missed an opportunity to put in a good word for him. Turnock was not the only man he'd shielded and it was this protective attitude toward his subordinates that made him such a popular and respected head of the Arabian desk.

"Ben-Gurion has obviously taken a leaf out of Churchill's

book," Deakin continued. " 'Give us the tools and we will do the job'; that is what he must have told the French, and one can understand why they couldn't resist the proposition. Here was the answer to all their prayers for, at one stroke, they could topple Nasser, cut off the supply of surplus Egyptian arms to the Algerian rebels, and restore the Suez Canal to its rightful owners without dirtying their hands. There's also a hidden bonus, one we can be sure the French will not have overlooked. Eisenhower is in the middle of a reelection campaign and he won't do anything which might prejudice the Jewish vote."

Winter shook his head. "They're barking up the wrong tree if they think the pro-Israel lobby will influence the election result."

That had always been the Foreign Office view, and confirmation had recently come from an unexpected source. Within minutes of returning home from New York, Harry Lang had telephoned to invite him around for a drink. "It's vital I see you as soon as possible," he'd said in a voice so grim that for several awful moments, until he'd started talking about public opinion stateside, Winter had thought Harry had somehow discovered that he and Katherine were lovers.

"I tell you, George, the Americans are neither for nor against either the Arabs or the Jews."

"They just want us out of the Middle East," Deakin said flatly.

Winter found it difficult to quarrel with the observation, especially as it was also in line with Foreign Office opinion. From the moment Nasser had seized the waterway, Dulles had led Eden around by the nose, floating the idea of the Suez Canal Users Association on the tenth of September to dissuade the British and French from taking the dispute to the Security Council. And then, after the PM had swallowed the bait, he had dished the scheme three days later with his off-the-cuff remarks at a press conference: "The United States has no intention of joining Britain and France in forcing a convoy through the Canal and it is fantastic that anyone should wish to impose some undesirable regime on Egypt." No one in Whitehall had believed it was simply a political gaffe, if only because Dulles was too shrewd a lawyer to make that kind of elementary mistake.

Turnock said, "I hope to God we're not a party to this secret agreement between France and Israel."

Even though Turnock was closer to the truth than he imagined, Winter thought it was a little late in the day for pious hopes. It was because Bracecourt at the Foreign Office had tipped him off about the French having some secret deal going with the Israelis that he'd arranged for Bill to meet with his opposite numbers in Paris. He had hoped that Turnock would pick up a few snippets of information which would give the SIS an insight into the political maneuvering, but the French had been too clever by half. Instead of being coy, they had laid their cards on the table, a move which, with hindsight, seemed to indicate that they intended to draw the British into their conspiracy.

"If the Jews do attack Egypt and we go in to separate them, we'll be accused of collusion."

"I'm sure we wouldn't be so foolish, Bill," Winter said blandly, and then quickly sidetracked the issue. "What's the latest on Hungary, George?" he asked. "Any new developments?"

"Nothing that is likely to deflect the U.S. State Department." Deakin leaned forward and knocked out his pipe in the ashtray on Winter's desk. "Budapest is having a season of funerals. Seven generals, all victims of the '49 purge, are to be reburied this coming Saturday, a repeat performance of Lazlo Rajk's posthumous exoneration."

"Do the Americans know about it?"

"I'd be surprised if they didn't. Johnston, our man in the Legation, read about it in the newspapers." Deakin took out a leather pouch and began to refill his pipe with the dark tobacco. "The CIA are probably better informed than we are now. Trouble is, Johnston has been cut off from our field people since Hedley was thrown out of the country. Naturally, we're taking steps to remedy this."

"I'm glad to hear it," said Winter.

Deakin appeared not to hear him. "You could liken Hungary to a smoldering autumn bonfire," he continued serenely. "At present, there are only a few wisps of smoke to be seen, but there's a tremendous amount of heat being generated under those damp leaves and it's only a question of time before everything goes up in flames."

Time was one thing they didn't have. Deakin didn't know it yet but as from next Wednesday, the seventeenth of October, the Americans were going to find themselves out in the cold. There would be no communications through the usual channels and no leaks from the cabinet to Ambassador Aldrich. Winter had Bracecourt's word for that, and more besides. The decks were being cleared for action and those civil servants who were opposed to Eden's policy were either being sent on leave or denied access to the relevant files.

"It's a pity that Eden and Dulles dislike each other so intensely," Winter said.

"Yes indeed." Abbott felt constrained to say something if only to justify his presence to the other two men. Conscious that Deakin was now staring at him thoughtfully, he crossed one elegant leg over the other, almost dropping the manila folders as he did so but managing to grab them before they slipped off his lap. "I believe they fell out when Dulles wanted to go to the brink over Indochina and we refused to support him." They had clashed again at the Geneva Conference in 1954 when Eden had acted as the honest broker between East and West, and Dulles had been so angry that he'd packed his bags and gone home, but somehow he didn't think George would be frightfully interested to know that.

"Dulles is a very sick man," Winter said emphatically.

"So is Eden," Turnock murmured.

"No one is denying that, Bill. The difference is that Eden's fevers are attributable to the aftereffects of a botched operation on his prostate whereas Dulles has cancer and it's terminal."

Deakin said, "Herbert Hoover is his deputy at the State Department, isn't he, Charles?"

"He is, but I don't think it will make much difference to us. The current betting is that Hoover will take the same line." Winter picked up a pencil and drew a series of interlocking circles on the blotting pad. "Perhaps we should forget Dulles and concentrate on Eisenhower instead," he said idly.

"Concentrate on Eisenhower?" Deakin echoed. "What exactly does that mean?"

Winter looked up. George might be mystified but not Miles Abbott. The alert expression on his face showed that he knew he'd been given the green light to set the operation in motion, one that would guarantee Eisenhower and Dulles did not attempt to interfere when the Anglo-French forces invaded Egypt. All he had to do now was conceal his intentions from the other two.

"I'm talking about the gentle art of persuasion, George," he said disarmingly. "If we are going to make Eisenhower see reason, we must hit him with some hard intelligence on Soviet contingency plans."

"We don't have any."

"Then get it."

Deakin struck a match and puffed at his pipe. "You're not suggesting that we manufacture the evidence, are you?" he said, raising his shaggy eyebrows.

Manufacturing the evidence was Abbott's job and it had nothing to do with Soviet contingency plans.

"Give me credit for some intelligence, George," Winter said irritably. "What's the use of faking information if the material won't stand up under examination? No, we've got to redouble our efforts and use every means at our disposal." He clenched his fist around the pencil and thumped the desk, a piece of theater to emphasize his words. "We must get the wireless intercept people to go through their transcripts to see if we've missed any clues along the way."

He could see from their faces exactly what Deakin and Turnock thought of his suggestion. A fighting speech by the new boy who was resorting to bluster because he didn't know what to do, which was precisely what he wanted them to believe. Katherine Lang had often said that it was difficult to tell when he was sincere or just acting a part; whilst scarcely a flattering remark, at this particular moment it was a comfort to know that there were times when even his mistress couldn't see through him.

"We'll do our best," said Deakin. Not to be outdone, Turnock nodded vigorously.

"Good. No man could ask for more." Winter switched on a frank smile to show that he had every confidence in them. "Now I think it's time we broke for lunch," he said jovially.

It was also time for Abbott to get in touch with Hedley, but there was no need to tell him so. Miles had been briefed beforehand and knew the score.

One of the best features of the second floor apartment at 22 Gresham Square was the sitting room. Large, high-ceilinged, and typically Edwardian in style from the ornate chandelier to the open fireplace with marble surrounds, its two sash-cord windows offered a commanding view of the small park below and the approach road to Kensington High Street. The park, a small oasis of lawn, flower beds, and stunted plane trees enclosed by iron railings, was strictly for residents only. Every tenant in the cul-de-sac possessed a key to the main gate which meant that, with the exception of two gardeners who tended the flower beds and mowed the grass, no outsider could gain admittance. An aerial photograph of Gresham Square revealed that it was shaped like an old-fashioned keyhole and with Number 22 strategically placed in the middle of the loop, Hedley could see why the SIS had leased the apartment. Even assuming they had lavish resources at their command, any opposition group who wanted to keep the house under discreet but close surveillance would find themselves confronted with a well-nigh insuperable problem.

During the week he'd lived there, Hedley had become familiar with the pattern of activity in the square. The postman made three deliveries a day, the first at 7:30 in the morning,

44

the second toward noon, and the last at four o'clock. Two milkmen served the neighborhood, one from Unigate, the other from Express Dairies, and the trash collectors called on Wednesdays. Most of the residents had their newspapers popped through the letter box; those who didn't collected theirs from the newsstand near the Underground station in the High Street on their way to work. There were other tradesmen and council employees who put in a brief appearance from time to time: road sweepers, gas and electricity inspectors, door-to-door salesmen, TV repairmen, and the like, but they were all legitimate as far as he could tell. At 1:30 that particular afternoon the square was deserted, probably because of the heavy rain.

The telephone called Hedley from the window. It rang four times, stopped, and then, exactly one minute later, trilled once more. It was, he thought, a lousy day to take a stroll but the summons left him with no choice. Donning a raincoat, he left the apartment and set off at a brisk walk toward Kensington High Street.

Although he was not supposed to use the same public call box on consecutive days, Hedley made straight for the Underground station. Abbott wouldn't think to question where he was phoning from; Miles would hear the coins go down when he pressed the button and that would be enough to satisfy him. Finding an empty booth, he picked up the telephone and dialed a number on the Bayswater exchange. Moments later, a muffled voice said, "Four Square Laundry at your service," and responding with the appropriate key phrase, Hedley pressed the call button.

Abbott said, "We've been given the green light for phase one, James."

"Starting when?"

"As from now." Abbott cleared his throat. "Any sign of the opposition?" he asked hesitantly, as if embarrassed to raise the subject.

"If they're around I haven't seen them."

"How very awkward. Maybe you'd better let the dog see the rabbit. You follow me, James?"

Hedley said he did. They had discussed how he should trail his coat when Abbott had briefed him the previous day. After observing the usual security precautions, they had met for lunch in a private room at the Connaught Hotel where Miles had given him his instructions. "It's a black operation," he'd said, wrinkling his nose, "and a very distasteful one, but we hope it won't be necessary to go the whole hog."

"All right, James," Abbott said briskly. "Call me when you've completed phase one, and try to make it as near five o'clock as you can. Don't forget to use the first fallback number."

"I won't."

"Good. Do you have any questions?"

"Only one," said Hedley. "What happened to that report I filed on Tuesday?"

"What report?"

"On my day trip to the seaside," he said evasively.

"Oh, that one." Abbott chuckled. "Didn't I tell you? The subject is dead and buried, old boy."

Hedley wasn't surprised. The previous Thursday evening when Miles had called around to the flat to show him the Court of Inquiry proceedings, he'd suspected that Winter had some ulterior motive for reopening the Crabb investigation. Obviously the snapshots allegedly taken in Kronshtadt hadn't bothered Winter one bit and the post office box number where he was required to send his report had been just a blind. Winter had sent him down to Portsmouth for one reason and one reason only: to put him through the hoop to see how well he performed in the field.

"When do I get the chit?" he asked.

"Chit?" Abbott repeated. "What are you talking about?"

"The one that says I passed the test with flying colors, Miles."

Hedley put the phone down without waiting for a reply and left the call box. Making for the bookstall, he bought a street guide to London and the outer suburbs and then walked out of the station. From Lytton's Self Drive garage in Abbingdon Crescent 200 yards down the road, he hired a white Ford Consul

46

and drove back to Gresham Square. Parking the car outside the apartment house, he went inside and made himself a cup of coffee and a sandwich.

Although neither thirsty nor hungry, it helped to pass the time while he allowed the dog to see the rabbit. Nobody had tailed him from the station, but that didn't mean to say that the opposition weren't around. If they had any sense, they would keep the cul-de-sac under observation from a stakeout in the High Street and assuming that supposition was correct, they would have spotted the white Ford Consul when he turned into Gresham Square. At 2:45, having worked out his route and satisfied that he had given the opposition sufficient notice to make their preparations, he left the flat for the second time.

Turning right on Kensington High Street, Hedley drove to Hammersmith Broadway and from there into Fulham Palace Road. The green Morris Oxford first appeared in his rearview mirror shortly before Putney Bridge and it was still there, two cars back but dogging him faithfully, when he headed south on the Portsmouth road. Seemingly anxious not to lose sight of the Ford Consul in Kingston, the driver made a hash of it and got too close. However, by the time they neared the mock-Tudor cottage set in ten acres of woodland on the outskirts of the suburb, he was back where he belonged, fifty yards to the rear with a butcher's delivery van between them.

The cottage lay well back in the grounds, invisible from the road. Hedley would have shot past it but for the white pole across the entrance to the long, winding driveway. Stopping the car just short of it, he got out, raised the barrier, and then drove on up to the house.

The gray-haired lady who answered the door viewed him with some suspicion until he told her he was an author and produced an introductory letter from the literary agency of Black and Littlejohn to prove it. His story sounded convincing and since it happened to correspond to the historical facts as she knew them, it never entered her head that the letter might be a forgery. Warming to Hedley, she took him on a guided tour of the house, pausing in one of the tiny bedrooms upstairs to point out the footpath through the woods that led, via a wicket gate in the high wooden fence, to the thirteenth hole of the golf course behind the property. That she then insisted on him staying to tea was an unexpected bonus.

Janet Roscoe went through the notes she had taken down over the telephone and after some deliberation decided to consult Tom McNulty. Clutching her notebook, she walked across the room, tapped on the communicating door and receiving a monosyllabic grunt, entered the adjoining office.

McNulty was poring over a thick brief, his elbows on the desk, his head supported between his hands, the palms of which were clapped over both ears. A cigar smoldered unheeded in the ashtray and for some moments he seemed unaware of her presence.

"You have to hand it to those boys in State." McNulty sighed and looked up, a wry smile on his face. "They never seem to suffer from writer's cramp. If they can use three words where one would suffice, you can bet your shirt they will."

"That's some brief you've got there," Janet murmured sympathetically. "Would you like me to come back when you're not so busy?"

"Hell, no. This dossier can wait." McNulty rippled the pages with his thumb. "It's just a summary of the Security Council meeting on the ninth of October and, believe me, it's dull." His eyes darted from the report to the notebook she was clutching to her chest. "Something tells me that Hedley has been on the move again," he said in a dry voice.

Janet nodded. "He left the apartment shortly after 1:30 today and made a telephone call from one of the booths of the Underground station in Kensington High Street. He then hired a Ford Consul from Lytton's Garage in Abbingdon Crescent and returned to Gresham Square. Twenty minutes later he got back into the car and drove out to Kingston where he spent approximately ninety minutes talking to the owner of Telegraph Cottage before making another telephone call from a box in Putney."

48

"Did you say Telegraph Cottage?" McNulty asked sharply.

"Yes. Do you know the place?"

"I've heard of it." McNulty scowled and crushed the cigar stub in the ashtray, grinding it to pieces. "It was Eisenhower's hideaway during the war. Captain Harry Butcher, his press aide, found the cottage for him when he and Ike were staying at the Dorchester. Ike would go there whenever he wanted some peace and quiet. The cottage was a haven, somewhere he could relax with his personal staff."

"I don't get it," said Janet. "Why should Hedley be interested in the cottage?"

"He probably isn't. My guess is that Winter sent him. He must have been briefed by Abbott when they lunched at the Connaught yesterday. And it looks to me as if they're after the same material some of the Taft people wanted to use against Ike when he was running for the Republican nomination in '52."

Janet frowned. "That should ring a bell, but it doesn't."

"Eisenhower had a very special driver," McNulty said slowly. "An Irish girl called Kay Summersby. There's a story buried in the Pentagon files that he wanted to divorce Mamie and marry her."

6.

Some truths are self-evident, but the old axiom that the shortest distance between two points is a straight line scarcely applied to Leconfield House, for although less than a mile from 54 Broadway, it could well have been on another planet as far as most of the SIS were concerned.

The reason was simple enough. Leconfield House belonged to MI5, the counterespionage people whom Deakin had nicknamed the "Headhunters," a subtle "in" joke which accurately described their function in life while implying they were on the same intellectual level as the wild men of Borneo. Some of his colleagues were even more disparaging; those who remembered the chaotic setup at Wormwood Scrubs in the early days of the war still regarded them as a bunch of incompetent amateur sleuths. For their part, MI5 maintained that, with Burgess and Maclean in Moscow and a large question mark against Kim Philby, the SIS were about as leakproof as a colander. As for efficiency, they had only to mention "Buster" Crabb and raise their eyebrows to ram the point home. In such a climate of mutual hostility, it followed that there was very little cooperation or contact between officers of the two Intelligence services, with certain notable exceptions, amongst them Malcolm Cleaver and Charles Pelham Winter.

Malcolm Cleaver had joined MI5 in the wake of the Wormwood Scrubs disaster, when much of the untidy filing system had been destroyed in an air raid and it was discovered that some of the microfilm records held elsewhere were indecipherable. A former Detective Superintendent, his transfer from the Metropolitan Police was said to have been greeted with a profound sigh of relief from the criminal fraternity who'd had good reason to fear him. A Churchillian figure with the same pugnacious features, Cleaver was noted for his shrewd intelligence, dogged perseverance, and his Lancashire accent which he'd retained despite living in London for the past thirty-five years.

No two men could have had less in common than Winter, a product of the elitist system of education, and Cleaver, the elementary schoolboy who'd started work in a cotton mill at the age of fourteen, but in their respective trades they had few equals and their unlikely friendship was founded on mutual respect. Over the years, they had come to trust one another completely, and Cleaver knew that he had only to pick up the telephone and ask for Winter's assistance to get it without going through the usual channels. Moreover, it was also clearly understood that any request was off the record, a verbal and reciprocal agreement that had prompted Winter to pay a visit to Leconfield House.

"I understand congratulations are in order," Cleaver said as they shook hands. "How does it feel to be one rung from the top of the ladder?"

"I suffer from vertigo, Malcolm," Winter said tersely. "I could fall off any time."

"Well, in that case, I've got just what the doctor ordered." Cleaver waved him to a chair and then produced a bottle of brandy and two glasses from the bottom drawer of his desk. "Courvoisier," he said, pouring two large tots into each glass. "Nothing like it for putting wool in your socks."

Winter picked up his glass and inspected the amber-colored liquid. "Trouble is, Malcolm, I'm not sure the ladder is all that safe either. It could be infected with dry rot."

"Hedley?" Cleaver raised a quizzical eyebrow. "Has he been feeding you duff information for the past two years?"

"Not that I'm aware of."

"Well, if I were in your shoes and had any doubts at all, I'd put him out to grass. The press aren't on to his little secret yet, and even supposing some bright correspondent does put two and two together Hedley will deny that he ever worked for the SIS. Bent or straight, he has to do that, otherwise he's of no use to Moscow or we get him under the Official Secrets Acts. I know it leaves a nasty taste in the mouth, but let's face it, you can't afford any more bad publicity."

Bracecourt had suggested to him that this was just what the KGB had in mind, that Hedley's expulsion order was part of a plan to discredit the SIS, but he'd dismissed the idea for two very good reasons. Even assuming that Hedley was bent, which seemed highly unlikely, it was wasteful to sacrifice a double agent to such little purpose, and from experience he knew the men in Dzerzhinsky Square were an unimaginative lot.

"So what's your problem, Charles?"

Winter stared at the window, turning the question over in his mind. Cleaver's office was a small back room on the top floor and all he could see were slate roofs, chimney pots, and a forest of television aerials, a view that was somewhat less than inspiring.

"We're going to resolve the Suez problem by force," he said slowly. "That's probably been our intention all along."

"If we do it'll split the nation from top to bottom, and the Third World will raise cain in the United Nations. You mark my words: we may go in roaring like a lion, but we'll come out again like a whipped dog with its tail between its legs." Cleaver swallowed his brandy and burped. "Still, that's Eden's problem, not yours."

Winter shook his head. "I'm running a black operation, Malcolm." He did not add that he had no official authority to do so. Mostly it was his own idea, although it was true to say that Bracecourt had prodded him into action: "Dulles or Eisenhower, you've got to make one of them bend or we're done for."

He'd said it over and over again, in different places, at different times.

"Black operations were all very well in wartime, but not now, Charles. You could get your fingers badly burned."

"Maybe." Winter took a gulp of brandy and then set his glass down on Cleaver's desk. "Off the record, Malcolm," he said brusquely, "how is Special Branch placed these days? Do they have any spare capacity?"

"Not unless we rob Peter to pay Paul."

"That's a pretty evasive answer," Winter said with a faint smile.

"It was a pretty vague question."

"All right, I'll be specific. What level of surveillance do you have on the Egyptian and Soviet embassies?"

"Blanket cover," said Cleaver. "Right across the board."

Blanket cover was the highest level of surveillance there was. It meant that, apart from examining every letter addressed to the embassies and posted within the UK, all incoming calls would be monitored, all visitors would be discreetly photographed for future identification, and additional officers would be assigned to beef up the watch on known Intelligence agents on the staff. In theory, these security arrangements were all-embracing; in practice, there were several loopholes virtually impossible to plug. The number of Intelligence officers on the staff varied from embassy to embassy. The amateur spies from the Armed Services were easy to identify because they were listed. The professionals were an altogether different kettle of fish; they were hidden amongst the Cultural, Labour, Commercial, and Agricultural Secretaries, which made life difficult for Special Branch. The Egyptians had one Naval, two Air, and one Assistant Military Attaché but only one known Secret Service officer, a Mr. Abdul Aziz Rida who masqueraded as a Second Secretary. It was much more difficult to keep tabs on the Soviet Embassy, whose staff numbered several hundred and where the KGB were known to have placed their agents amongst the chauffeurs, secretaries, clerks, and archivists, as well as the more senior grades. No less than six men working in shifts were needed to keep one Intelligence agent under surveillance and since Special Branch had only 400 officers on strength, the Soviet Embassy alone stretched their resources to near breaking point. Given this manpower limitation, it was inevitable that some of the smaller fish would slip through the net.

Winter said, "About this black operation of mine . . ."

Cleaver raised a hand to silence him before he went any further. "No offense intended," he said politely, "but I'd rather you didn't tell me."

"And no need to be alarmed, Malcolm. I wasn't about to give you any details. It's just that there is a strong pro-Arab lobby in Whitehall and I'd like to know the names of those who might be inclined to put conscience before country."

"You want a list of visitors to the Egyptian Embassy in South Audley Street, is that it?"

Winter nodded. "From today onward," he added.

"You've got it." Cleaver reached for the bottle and topped up both their glasses. "Of course, you do realize we'll only be skimming the surface? I mean, your worm in the apple could contact Mr. Abdul Aziz Rida through an intermediary. Come to that, he could meet him on neutral ground; never a night goes by but what there's some diplomatic function."

"You're so right," said Winter. "That's why I wanted to know how Special Branch was placed."

"I take it you have a target in mind?" said Cleaver.

"Several targets."

"Then you'll have to do some pruning. Six, maybe eight officers is all I can manage, and they won't be available until Monday."

"Fair enough." Winter flipped open a small notebook and uncapped his fountain pen. "Let's start with these two," he said, printing their names in block capitals.

Yesterday they had used a green Morris Oxford to shadow him; today they had switched to a gray '52 model Standard Vanguard. They had also changed their tactics; instead of lying back they had sat on his tail all the way across town from Kensington to Bishopsgate. Even when Hedley was clear of London and heading northeast on the A 10, they hadn't bothered to drop back. It was as if they had been determined to let him know that he was being tailed, or so it had seemed until he'd stopped for lunch at a roadhouse beyond Ware. Declining to follow him into the parking lot, they'd driven straight past the roadhouse to pull into a rest area farther on.

They had tucked in behind the Ford Consul again when he'd left the pub an hour later, sticking to him like glue until he turned off the main road north of Standon. Then, inexplicably, they'd started to act coy, dropping farther and farther back to the point where, on several occasions, he had been unable to see them in the rearview mirror. He'd slowed down each time it happened, often crawling along at twenty miles an hour before they decided to catch up with him again. It was a childish game which they'd kept up even though the bends in the road became much more pronounced beyond the village of Stocking Welham and there were any number of unmarked lanes branching off into the Hertfordshire countryside where he could have lost them.

Approaching Little Stocking, Hedley glanced into the rearview mirror for the umpteenth time and catching a glimpse of the Vanguard, signaled that he was turning right into the dirt road leading to Wyecroft Farm.

The farmhouse was a hybrid of Tudor crossed with Elizabethan plus a latticework of gutterings and drainpipes that had been added before World War I. Seen from a distance, the white stucco walls, external oak beams, leaded windows, and slate roof were not unattractive, but the closer Hedley got to the farmhouse, the more dilapidated it began to look. Some of the slates were missing and, as he got out of the car, he noticed that a large chunk of plaster had come away from the wall on the right-hand side of the front porch.

Pausing long enough to clean some of the mud off his shoes on the metal scraper outside, he walked into the porch and rang the bell. There were no melodic chimes, just a low-pitched buzzing sound made by a flat battery. A tarnished brass knocker appeared to be the only other means of communication, but before he could use it, the door was opened by a small, almost bald-headed man wearing a pair of baggy, work-stained slacks and a much-darned sweater of indeterminate color.

"Major Flaxman?" Hedley inquired politely.

"That's me. You must be Hedley. Been expecting you." He opened the door wider. "Better come inside."

Hedley stepped past him into the shadowy hall, giving his shoes another wipe on the doormat as he did so. "It's very kind of you to spare me the time," he said.

"Not at all, Hedley." Flaxman closed the door and then gave it a sharp kick. "Damn thing keeps sticking," he muttered. "Must oil it sometime."

"Should do the trick." Hedley smiled; the major's habit of using short staccato sentences was beginning to rub off on him.

"We can talk in here." Flaxman opened a door off the hall and ushered him inside. "My study," he said, as if the chaos was something to be proud of.

The desk under the window was littered with scraps of paper and back numbers of *Farmer's Weekly*, some of which were stacked in an untidy pile. Other periodicals, mainly *The Field* and *Country Life*, occupied the seat of the only easy chair in the room. There was a film of dust on the telephone, the faded curtains hung in limp folds, and the whole room, like its owner, seemed in need of attention.

The study was at the front of the house, directly opposite the dirt lane. A hedge concealed the road to Little Stocking, and for all Hedley knew, the Standard Vanguard could have driven straight past the farm. However, he was sure they had seen him turn right, in which case it was virtually impossible to miss the sign in the grass verge that pointed the way to Wye-croft Farm. All they had to do then was drive into the village and ask one of the shopkeepers who owned the farmhouse.

"You've got a nice view," Hedley said, conscious that the major was watching him curiously.

"Not bad." Flaxman swept the magazines off the chair on to the floor so that Hedley could sit down. "Of course, it's better

56

in spring and summer. Lots of wild flowers in the hedgerows and the elm trees in full leaf. Not that I get much time to admire the view. Farming is an all-year-round job."

"How many acres do you have under cultivation?" It seemed only polite to ask.

"Eighty-five. The soil in these parts is good for peas, potatoes, and sugar beet. Then there are the pigs and chickens." Flaxman sucked his teeth. "Still, I manage to take the odd day off to go hunting."

"Really?"

"Winter tell you I'm the MFH around here?"

Hedley shook his head. The biographical details Abbott had passed on to him were brief and to the point. Flaxman had served fifteen years in the army before resigning his commission in the Eleventh Hussars to take up farming. In an otherwise unremarkable career, he had been one of Eisenhower's military aides when the general was Supreme Commander of NATO forces from 1950 to 1952.

"Surprised at that," said Flaxman. "Mind you, Winter has always been a bit absentminded. Cousin of mine, you know."

"Is he really? How very interesting."

"Yes. Well, blood's thicker than water, I always say. That's why I'm prepared to help him out." Flaxman opened the bottom drawer of his desk and brought out a large, leather-bound volume. "This is what you're after," he said. "Complete record of every social engagement and official visit made by General Eisenhower while he was at NATO Headquarters."

"These are his personal diaries from '50 to '52?"

"Mine," said Flaxman. "It was my job to keep a duplicate record of Ike's engagements. By rights, I should have handed them in when I left Versailles, but they got packed in with my gear and I decided to hang on to them. Thought they would make a nice souvenir so I had them bound together."

Hedley weighed the volume in one hand. "There must be enough material here for a book," he said thoughtfully.

"You mean up here." Flaxman tapped his forehead. "I did think about writing a book, but never had the time or the patience to buckle down to it. A great man, the general. Often went riding with him and enjoyed the occasional round of golf."

"I understand he's a pretty good bridge player too," Hedley said, making small talk.

Flaxman peered at him suspiciously. "I'm not boring you, am I?" he asked.

"Good Lord, no."

"Just as well—can't stand bores myself." He frowned. "Funny thing is, I only saw Eisenhower once during the war. The Victory Parade in Tunis—he was on the reviewing stand with Monty and that girl driver of his. What was her name now?"

"Kay Summersby."

"That's right. Pretty little thing, though she must be getting on for fifty now."

In fact, Kay Summersby was forty-eight but Hedley thought it unwise to correct him. Although Flaxman didn't seem very bright, it might occur to him to ask how he knew.

"Her ex-husband was in publishing. Alice did tell me that she was a fashion model for Worth of Paris just before the war."

"I'm sorry," said Hedley, "but who's Alice?"

Flaxman seemed genuinely astonished that he didn't know. "My elder sister," he explained. "They came out in the same season. She said there was a lot of talk about Ike having an affair with Kay. Absolute rubbish, of course, but I understand it was in all the American newspapers."

"I bet."

"Muckraking." Flaxman stared at him, a thoughtful expression on his face. "That's not Winter's line, is it?" he asked sternly.

Suddenly the gallant major was not the buffoon he'd taken him for; it was clear to Hedley that behind Flaxman's bluff exterior there was a shrewd brain.

"Of course it isn't," he lied, straight-faced. "I can't tell you why he wants these diaries, but rest assured it has nothing to do with Kay Summersby."

It had everything to do with Kay Summersby—and that was the most unpalatable part of Winter's concept. Hedley had been persuaded that it was a necessary evil, but that didn't mean to say he enjoyed dirtying his hands.

"Good. That's all I want to know." Flaxman slapped his knees and then launched himself from the chair. "Just tell Winter I'd like them back when he's finished with them."

Hedley was only too glad to take the hint and go. Flaxman muttered something about it being a pleasure to have met him, but his voice lacked conviction and his parting handshake was decidedly limp.

Vasili Korznikov accepted a glass of wine from a passing waitress and deliberately turned his back on Abdul Aziz Rida. He knew the Egyptian wanted to get him in a quiet corner, but Rida would have to be patient. The cocktail party at the Yugoslavian Embassy was in honor of a visiting trade delegation, and with Bracecourt among the guests, it was only prudent that he should be seen talking to some of his hosts. Apart from discretion and good manners, it was also a fact that Ambassador Malik had reminded his staff that Comrade Khrushchev was anxious to establish cordial relations with Marshal Tito, and they were therefore expected to do their bit.

Korznikov glanced around the salon, spotted Dr. Petar Tomic talking to a group of people at the far end of the room and although he didn't know the Economic Counselor all that well, decided to join them. As he started to ease his way through the crush, somebody tapped him on the shoulder. Turning about, Korznikov found himself face to face with Jehan Rida.

"Why the stern expression, Vasili?" she said teasingly, after he'd greeted her. "Aren't you pleased to see me?"

"Of course I am," he said, and meant it. Jehan Rida was a very attractive woman, the kind of sensuous type he instinctively undressed with his eyes, although on this occasion, the low-cut dress left very little to the imagination.

"Then perhaps it is my husband you wish to avoid?" she said with an impish smile.

"Careful," he warned. "Bracecourt is watching us."

"Bracecourt?"

"The small blond man in the dark suit and blue tie standing near the portrait of Marshal Tito."

"Ah yes, I see him," she said and looked away. "Is he a spy?"

"Need you ask? He works for the British Foreign Office. Until he leaves the party, I would rather not approach your husband."

"But he might stay to the end."

"That would be very inconsiderate of him."

"Would you like me to distract him?"

Korznikov thought it over. The Englishman was reputed to be fond of the ladies, and Jehan certainly knew how to turn on the charm. He could have wished for a neutral ally, but one of the curious things he'd noticed about the English was their lack of hostility toward the Egyptians. Had their positions been reversed, he would have immediately smelled a rat whereas Bracecourt would undoubtedly be extremely civil to her, perhaps even flattered that such an attractive woman should seek him out.

"All right, but don't make it too obvious." He smiled. "Talk to somebody else first."

"That's just what I planned to do, Vasili."

"Good. In the meantime, I'm going to have a few words with Dr. Petar Tomic."

"Don't be too long," she murmured.

Korznikov did not trust himself to watch Jehan as she moved away. The sight of her rounded buttocks undulating beneath the skintight dress would be enough to arouse the wildest sexual fantasies with all too predictable and visible results. Instead, he thought about his wife Olga back home in Leningrad, whose lumpy body and coarse features never failed to cool his ardor. Fixing a smile on his face, he gravitated toward the far end of the room.

A brief handshake with Dr. Tomic and a cheery greeting was sufficient to establish himself within the circle. Thereafter, Korznikov merely went through the motions, his face set in a thoughtful expression as if deeply interested in the conversation going on around him. From where he positioned himself it was possible to keep an eye on Bracecourt, and presently he saw Jehan Rida move toward the Foreign Office man, a glass of tomato juice in one hand, a cigarette in the other.

Bracecourt reacted in exactly the way he'd predicted. Courteous and slightly withdrawn at first, the Englishman gradually thawed and became quite animated, captivated by Jehan and her charms which, as she moved in closer, he could hardly avoid. Once satisfied that Bracecourt had eyes for no one else Korznikov backed away from Dr. Tomic's group, deposited his now empty wineglass on the tray of a passing waitress and, politely declining the offer of another drink, began to make an exit. He moved slowly from group to group, exchanging a few brief words, so that it took him all of ten minutes to reach the main hall. Crossing it in a few strides, he opened a door directly opposite the salon and entered the small library which the Yugoslavs had put at his disposal. Moments later, Rida joined him.

Rida bore such a close resemblance to Major Salah Salem that Korznikov had often wondered if they were related, except that he couldn't envisage Rida dancing round a bonfire in his underpants to woo the Sudanese, or anyone else for that matter. The Egyptian Intelligence officer might be a bundle of nervous energy, but he was far too dignified to make an exhibition of himself.

Without any preamble, Rida said, "I've received some very disturbing information."

"So I gathered." Korznikov sat down on the leather sofa, masking his curiosity behind an air of indifference.

"It comes from an unimpeachable source, Vasili," Rida said, determined to impress his Soviet counterpart.

"Direct?"

"Through an intermediary who called at the embassy this morning, ostensibly to ask for a visa."

"Then it's secondhand and open to doubt."

"I don't think so. The intermediary is a man of some standing with influential friends in Whitehall. He said there was a move afoot to persuade President Eisenhower to change America's foreign policy, particularly with regard to the Suez Canal dispute; that pressure would be exerted to achieve this."

"Pressure?" Korznikov repeated thoughtfully. "What sort of pressure? Reasoned argument or the usual anti-Soviet propaganda concerning our alleged designs on the Middle East?"

"The British have already tried both those lines and failed." Rida rubbed his hands together as if washing them under a tap. "Although he was unable to give any specific details, the intermediary did say his friend had reason to believe the SIS were mounting a special operation."

"Special meaning black." Korznikov frowned. "That's Winter's trademark."

"Winter?"

"Charles Pelham Winter, Head of Administration, and a high flier. It wouldn't surprise us if he ended up running the SIS one of these days."

The KGB had a dossier on Winter, mostly background stuff but interesting reading for all its trivia. "Date and place of birth: Winchester, May 10, 1912. Educated at Eton and Oxford. Commissioned into Coldstream Guards in 1939, evacuated from Dunkirk, seconded to Special Operations, entered MI6 through back door after brilliant wartime record with counterintelligence." The details were all there on microfilm and he knew them by heart. "Married the Honorable Geraldine Montague in 1938. Two issues—son, aged seventeen, now in last year at Eton; daughter, fifteen, at Roedean. Most intimate friends—Mr. and Mrs. H. Lang, Chalfont Avenue, Regents Park."

"It's essential to know your enemy," he said aloud.

"Does this Winter have any firsthand experience of the Middle East?" Rida asked.

"He's never been stationed outside Europe."

"Then he's not our shy informant."

A man who knew the Middle East, a man who was possibly more Arab than the Arabs? The desert and the nomadic way of life had a curious effect on a certain kind of Englishman. Lawrence of Arabia was not unique, he was just the first of many; some famous like Glubb, Burroughs, and St. John Philby, others virtually unknown outside the tiny desert sheikdoms they had helped to create.

"You must tell the intermediary that you want to meet this shy well-wisher, Aziz."

"Impossible, Vasili, he'll never agree to it."

"Send a message to him," Korznikov continued. "Say that you must have specific information. Do that and we will be able to help you."

"But . . ."

"No buts, Aziz—just arrange to meet him on neutral ground. Pick some minor diplomatic function at one of the nonaligned embassies, or better still, persuade your Swedish friend to give an intimate dinner party."

"Yes—that's a possibility." Rida brightened visibly. "In fact, I'm almost sure it'll work."

"I'm quite certain it will." Kornikov glanced at his wristwatch. "Now I think it's time you rescued your wife, Aziz. We don't want to arouse Bracecourt's suspicions, do we?"

Rida nodded. "Are you coming too?" he asked.

"No, I think it's best if I slip away from the party. You run along and enjoy yourself."

Korznikov leaned back and clasped both hands behind his neck. He thought the future looked very rosy. Rida didn't know it, but he was about to recruit another agent for the Soviet Union. No doubt the shy Englishman who had sought to warn the Egyptians did not regard himself as a traitor, but traitor he was. He had crossed the dividing line and was already beyond the point of no return, an unpleasant fact of life which would be spelled out to him in no uncertain terms when the time was ripe. Perhaps what gave him the most pleasure was the knowledge that he'd set the whole thing up right under Bracecourt's nose.

Korznikov's assumption was not wholly correct. Although Bracecourt hadn't seen him leave the salon, others had. Amongst the English guests from the Board of Trade and Wellcraft Engineering Limited was a man called Lovell. Most of the officials from the Board of Trade thought Lovell belonged to Wellcraft Engineering, the Yugoslavs believed he was with the Board of Trade, while the Managing Director of Wellcraft assumed he was just another bloody civil servant. All three deductions were wrong.

Lovell was one of the Special Branch officers whose task it was to monitor the Yugoslav community in London, diplomats and dissidents alike. As luck would have it, Lovell had been listening to Dr. Petar Tomic expounding on his country's economy when Korznikov had approached the diplomat and introduced himself. The Russian's name had meant nothing to Lovell, but he had a retentive memory. He was also extremely observant. Shortly after Korznikov had made his exit, he had observed a dark-haired Egyptian sneaking out of the salon like a thief in the night. He was also able to recall that this same man had arrived with a sensuous bit of goods who subsequently he'd noticed deep in conversation with Bracecourt at the time her husband or whatever had done the old vanishing act.

7.

Winter stopped outside the office and glanced up at the two-way illuminated sign built into the wall above the door. It was only an oblong-shaped panel divided in two, one half colored red, the other green, and the words Engaged and Enter painted on the glass, but this somewhat ugly-looking gadget was visible proof of his new status. Even so, it was a strange experience to open the door and walk into the Deputy Controller's office without having to wait for the green light to come on.

Shedding his raincoat, he hung it up in the cupboard and then sat down at the desk. Although every trace of his predecessor had been removed over the weekend to make room for his own memorabilia, the photograph of Geraldine and the children in a silver frame, the cut-glass ashtray, the old-fashioned pen and inkstand that had once belonged to his father, and the engraved paper knife which Katherine and Harry had given him one Christmas were not enough to make him feel at home in his new surroundings. The red telephone, a direct line to Number 10 Downing Street, was particularly intimidating and he hoped it would remain silent until he'd found his feet. Uncertain which of the two buttons under the desk operated the engaged sign, he pressed the left-hand one and was childishly pleased when he saw the red light glowing in the panel.

A strident summons from one of the telephones dispelled his euphoria and caused a momentary flutter until he realized the incoming call was on the normal office extension and not the direct line to Downing Street.

Lifting the receiver, he automatically said, "Double five three," and then glancing at the dial, hastily corrected himself, "I mean five zero one."

"You had me worried for a moment," said Cleaver.

"A slip of the tongue, Malcolm."

"That's understandable. How do you like your new office?"

"To tell you the truth, I'm a little overawed, but I suppose I'll get used to it in time. What can I do for you?"

"Can we go to secure?" Cleaver asked.

"You bet." Winter depressed the button on the cradle and checked the black box on the floor. "I have a green light," he said.

"Me too." Cleaver hesitated as if unsure how to continue. "This new job of yours," he said presently, "will it make any difference?"

"Not as far as you're concerned, Malcolm. My old job has been trimmed down and I've kept the most important folios. When Edmunds, the commandant of our training wing, takes over as Head of Administration, he'll find he's little more than a totem pole."

"That's answered one question," said Cleaver. "Now for the other. Does the name Vasili Korznikov mean anything to you?"

"I can't say it does."

"Korznikov is a Trade Counselor. At least, that's what we had him pegged for until the Yugoslavs held a party for a visiting trade delegation on Friday night. Lovell was there posing as an official from the Board of Trade, and so was our friend, Mr. Abdul Aziz Rida."

Lovell had never laid eyes on Rida before, and but for the voluptuous lady on his arm, he would probably have spared the Egyptian no more than a passing glance. In Lovell's words, her

66

undoubted charms, so obviously on display, were enough to make all the other women there spit out their eyeteeth and draw the men like bees to honey pot. As if aware that she was not exactly popular with her own sex, she had gone out of her way to talk to all the unaccompanied males who happened to take her fancy. One of those she had favored had subsequently joined Lovell's group and introduced himself to Dr. Petar Tomic and the British guests as Vasili Korznikov.

"Apparently, Korznikov was a little too hail-fellow-well-met," Cleaver continued. "Anyway, Lovell has a nose for these things and he was convinced that our Russian friend was putting on an act and would bear watching. After ten minutes or so, Korznikov withdrew from the circle and gradually made his way toward the far end of the room when he then left the salon. The party was still in full swing and none of the other guests were ready to leave—with the exception of guess who?"

"Abdul Aziz Rida," said Winter. "Minus wife."

"Right. Lovell spotted her talking to Bracecourt, which didn't greatly surprise him since friend Bracecourt is a very handsome man. Nor at the time did he think it particularly odd that she'd apparently been deserted by her companion. However, Lovell began to see things in a different light when the Egyptian reappeared some twenty minutes later and he observed them finally get together again. The longer he watched them, the more convinced he became that she had been acting as a decoy. And so, like the good policeman he is, Lovell asked Bracecourt who she was."

"I take it Korznikov didn't return to the party?"

"He most certainly did not," Cleaver said emphatically.

Of the two, Winter believed Rida was the one who'd asked for the meet. Certainly, Lovell's account of the charade indicated that Korznikov had decided how and when it should take place. It was also on the cards that he had told Jehan Rida to keep Bracecourt occupied while they slipped out of the salon.

"I think you could be on to a big fish, Malcolm," Winter said eventually.

"Yes, that's how I see him."

"Now for the sob story."

"What sob story?"

"The one about your resources being overstretched," said Winter.

Half the KGB agents stationed in London belonged to the security section whose task was to maintain a continuous watch on everybody in the embassy, from the ambassador down to the lowliest clerk, for what was loosely described as "unhealthy signs." Because their activities were entirely directed against their own people, embassy security officers were given a low rating by MI5 and were not subjected to the same degree of surveillance that would be accorded to a KGB field agent. In the world of espionage, it was usual for like to deal with like, and since it had already been established that Abdul Aziz Rida was the top-ranking Egyptian Intelligence officer in London, it followed that Vasili Korznikov probably enjoyed equal status in the First Chief Directorate.

"Those two names you gave me on Friday," Cleaver said, feeling his way. "What do you have on them?"

"Not a damned thing," Winter admitted readily. "It's just that I'm running a delicate operation and it would have been nice to know which way they were going to jump."

"I'm afraid Korznikov has overriding priority."

"Is that another way of saying you intend to cancel our arrangement?"

"When did I ever welsh on you?" Cleaver demanded angrily.

"Offhand, I can't recall a single occasion."

"Damn right you can't, and I'm not about to do so now. I had eight men singled out for your job, but I'll need six of them to watch Korznikov."

"You're leaving me with two officers."

"Mathematics must be your strong suit," Cleaver said dryly. "How do you want them deployed?"

Winter closed his eyes and wondered how the hell he could deploy two Special Branch officers to any useful purpose when at least three times that number were required to keep one

68

target under surveillance. He supposed he could always ignore one of the suspects, but with no evidence to go on, how did he choose between them? On the toss of a coin? No, that would be a stupid way to resolve the problem. Covering both suspects for twelve hours out of the twenty-four was far from an ideal solution but it was better than putting all his eggs in one basket.

"I want to stay with both targets," he said crisply, "from six in the evening until six the following morning. Can you do that?"

"For how long?"

"Three weeks to a month. Of course, they'll have to work a different shift at weekends to cover as much of the daylight hours as we can."

"With a schedule like that," said Cleaver, "they'll be walking zombies before the week is out. When are they expected to rest?"

"Whenever you can find a volunteer from the off-duty personnel to relieve them."

Cleaver sighed. "You're a hard man, Charles."

"So I've been told."

"Chances are they'll be spotted."

"In that case, they'll serve as a deterrent." Winter put the phone down and, reaching under the desk for the left-hand button, switched off the Engaged sign. With almost perfect timing, somebody then tapped on the door and like a child with a new toy he took great delight in pressing the second button to illuminate the word Enter in a green light.

For a man who was usually most fastidious about his appearance, Miles Abbott looked singularly disheveled. His suit was creased in all the wrong places as if he had slept in it, and as he came nearer and placed a folder on his desk, Winter couldn't help noticing that his collar and shirt cuffs were decidedly grubby.

"You look as though you've had a few late nights," he observed mildly.

"Three on the trot." Abbott cupped a hand over his mouth to

69

stifle a yawn. His eyes were sore and red-rimmed and it was as much as he could do to keep them open. "Friday, Saturday, and Sunday."

"Sounds like a lost weekend."

"But not an unproductive one, I think."

Winter opened the folder that had been placed in front of him and glanced at the list of contents on the first page. "You've obviously done a lot of homework, Miles."

Abbott smiled wryly. Homework was scarcely the word he would have used to describe the hours he'd spent locked away inside a tiny room in the basement. "I spent Friday night and most of Saturday going through Flaxman's diaries looking for blank days, which I've listed on page 2 of the brief." Abbott saw Winter turn the page and moved around the desk to stand beside him. "I'm afraid they were very few and far between," he murmured apologetically.

"Just six dates." Winter looked up. "Is that all we've got to play with?"

"Well, Eisenhower has always been a glutton for work. I'm not saying he didn't take the odd vacation while he was at NATO Headquarters, but I decided to ignore the leave periods. Flaxman didn't record where the general had been or what he'd been doing. I suppose he figured it was none of his business, which of course it wasn't. Anyway, I didn't think those dates would look right because they were too bloody convenient. I mean, if this assignation we're arranging is to have any credibility, it must appear furtive."

"So we're left with these six days: two in May '51, one in September, another in November, plus two in March of the following year." Winter stroked his chin. "I wonder if we're wise to consider anything in '52? March is too close to the Republican convention and most people will find it hard to believe that Eisenhower would risk a scandal at that point in time."

"That's what I thought," said Abbott. "If you turn to page 3, you'll see that I have taken this factor into account when I constructed the scenario."

Although entirely fictitious, the scenario conveyed a ring of truth. The story began in March '51 with Eisenhower writing an affectionate letter to Kay Summersby, a sort of sentimental journey down memory lane to see if she still felt the same way about him. After a suitable interval of some three weeks, it was suggested that the general should write again expressing his joy at hearing from Kay and hinting that if she happened to be in France during the first two weeks in May, there was a very good chance they could see each other again. Abbott recommended that optimism should give way to disappointment when he learned that May was impossible, but that it should be rekindled by a postscript which left him in no doubt that he still held pride of place in her affections. The scenario then moved to its climax with two further letters from the general, one written in the middle of July suggesting a possible date in September, and the other toward the end of August detailing the arrangements that he'd made.

"This date you've picked in September," said Winter. "Will it hold up?"

"I think so. It's the day after Eisenhower visited the training center at Larzac, and Kay Summersby has very fond memories of the south of France. One thing I'm sure of: we can rely on Hedley to produce the necessary evidence."

"You've briefed him already?"

"Yes. As a matter of fact, he's on his way to Paris now. I've booked him into the Castiglione on the Rue Faubourg St. Honoré where one of our French colleagues will meet him early this afternoon."

"You really are on the ball, Miles."

Praise from Winter was such a rare occurrence that for a few moments Abbott was thown out of his stride. Embarrassed, he fingered the knot in his tie, then noisily cleared his throat. "Perhaps you'd like to approve the letters I've drafted?" Reaching across Winter with a murmured, "May I?" he found the appropriate page. "I think you'll find they mirror Eisenhower's style, the way he writes, the expressions he uses, and so on."

"I trust you haven't made them too sentimental?"

Abbott shook his head. "If anything, you may find them too offhand."

Winter could see what he meant as soon as he read the opening lines of a letter allegedly written on the tenth of March 1951. The prose was stilted, the style almost matter-of-fact, but that was Eisenhower's way of expressing himself on a personal level and the content struck exactly the right note.

"What about our penman?" Winter turned a page and went on reading. "Can he produce the goods?"

"You'll find a specimen of his handiwork in the folder," said Abbott. "I'm assured it's good enough to deceive Eisenhower himself, never mind the handwriting experts."

"What have you done about the stage props?"

The questions were coming thick and fast, but there was nothing unusual about that. Winter was one of the few men Abbott knew who was capable of absorbing a detailed brief while conducting an interrogation at one and the same time.

"I printed the letterheads myself yesterday afternoon. The notepaper has the same watermark as the stationery used by NATO Headquarters and we can age it after the penman has done his stuff. We're okay for envelopes, but we've still to make the woodcuts for the post office franking. I don't think we need to reproduce the APO number because I figure the general would never have mailed the letters through the U.S. Army Postal Service. The postage stamps won't be a problem. Philately is a hobby of mine and I can get a set of unfranked stamps from a dealer I know in Leicester Square."

"Good." Winter found a sheet of scrap paper in one of the drawers and uncapped his fountain pen. "These letters are okay, in fact they're first class, but we can do with a couple more to give the story greater depth."

The great love affair had actually died a sudden but natural death on the tenth of November 1945, when Eisenhower had left his headquarters in Frankfurt, never to return. From then on, Kay Summersby had only seen him once to speak to, and that was in his office in the Pentagon the following year, shortly before she had taken her discharge from the WACs. She had, however, been present, sitting unobtrusively at the back of the auditorium, when the general had addressed the Fellowship of United States and British Comrades at the Seventh Armory on Park Avenue in the fall of '48, and Winter thought it probable that she had also tried to see him during the time he was president of Columbia University.

A letter that Eisenhower might have sent to Kay Summersby around that time, explaining why it was impossible for him to see her again, would put the general in a very unfavorable light, Winter thought. A second note, written three years later in October '51, coldly severing their relationship forever, would put the final nail in his coffin.

"We need to create the impression that Eisenhower is a moral coward, Miles, a weak man who is motivated by expediency and self-interest. He acts the way he does not from personal convictions but out of fear of the consequences if he lets things slide." Winter laid his pen aside and handed the draft to Abbott. "Something on these lines should do the trick."

The writing was almost illegible, something Winter had in common with most doctors except that his prescription was intended to create distress rather than cure an illness.

Abbott pursed his lips. "It leaves a nasty taste in the mouth," he said.

"That's the whole idea, Miles. I don't like it any more than you do, but it has to be done. If we play our cards right, none of this business will come out in the open. Like you, I don't want to see anyone hurt."

Abbott hoped he meant it, but a doubt persisted. "There are a couple of other points that still bother me," he said slowly. "There's the matter of Hedley's expenses and the quarterly audit of the Imprest Account the day after tomorrow. Admittedly, they are only examining the account ending the thirtieth of September, but when it comes to reconciling the cash they'll have to look at the subsequent entries."

"Who's on the audit apart from the paymaster?"

73

"Bill Turnock."

"You needn't worry about Bill; he'll sign anything that's put in front of him."

"And the paymaster?"

"I'll whisper a few words in his ear." Winter pushed the folder toward Abbott, determined to bring their conversation to a close. "What was the other point?" he asked briskly.

"Well, it's the Americans. What do we say to them when they ask us how we came by these letters to Kay Summersby?"

"That's my problem," Winter said firmly. "Not yours."

No matter how big the problem, there was always a solution. For instance, he could lift the phone, call New York, and arrange a break-in, but that would mean drawing an outsider into the conspiracy and could prove dangerous. Given the need for secrecy, it was safer to ask the local office to supply a list of unsolved burglaries in Manhattan over the last two months and take it from there.

He waited until Abbott had closed the door behind him, then picked up the phone and rang Deakin. At the back of his mind he nursed a hope that somehow good old George would get them all off the hook.

Deakin was his usual calm, unemotional self. There had been some interesting developments in Budapest over the weekend. The funeral of the seven army officers, innocent victims of the '50 to '53 purges, had taken place on Saturday at the Farkasret Cemetery where they had been buried with full military honors. There had been no demonstrations by the large crowds but, significantly, Mihaly Farkas, the Minister of the Armed Forces and political chief of the AVH, had been arrested that same afternoon. Farkas was the man who had rigged the show trials, and the fact that public opinion had forced Erno Gerö and his colleagues into taking this extraordinary move could mean the government was on the point of collapse.

The bonfire seemed to be smoldering nicely; unfortunately for Winter the flames weren't in evidence yet.

* * *

The photographs lacked high definition, and any professional jealous of his reputation would have consigned them to the wastepaper basket. Some had been taken at night with an infrared camera, but the majority had been shot in daylight from a distance, using a wide-angle lens to capture the subject while he was on the move. In Janet Roscoe's opinion, none of the exposures flattered Hedley, but at least he was recognizable.

Of the batch of photographs arranged in date order on her desk Janet Roscoe was interested only in the ones that had been taken on Friday evening. In sequence, they showed Hedley waiting outside the Underground station in Sloane Square, getting into a taxicab that was already occupied, and then leaving it ten minutes later near the Globe theater on Shaftesbury Avenue. Closer examination of the first and second exposures revealed that Hedley was carrying a brown paper parcel, whereas in the third he was empty-handed. Earlier that same day Hedley had called on a certain Major Rupert Flaxman at Wyecroft Farm near Little Stocking and while it was pure guesswork she was convinced that the contents of the brown paper parcel had been supplied by him. It was a pity Kaplin's team hadn't stayed with the cab, although that was largely her fault because she had made it clear that Hedley was the prime target. But guessing again, she thought the unidentified passenger was Miles Abbott, a not unreasonable assumption, since only last Wednesday Abbott and Hedley had been seen together lunching at the Connaught Hotel.

They had been in touch again late on Saturday afternoon, she was sure, Hedley phoning him from a booth on Kensington High Street. According to Kaplin, their conversation had lasted all of fifteen minutes, a departure from their normal procedure which had puzzled her until this morning, when Hedley had checked into the West London Terminal. From there he'd boarded a coach for Heathrow and caught the 1105 BEA flight to Paris, a surprise development that had set the wires humming between the airport, Berkeley Square, and the American Embassy on Boissy d'Anglas. By the time Kaplin had finished describing Hedley's appearance and the clothes he was wearing the Paris office had had less than an hour in which to organize a reception committee.

"Relax, stop worrying," Kaplin had told her, "they'll be there." Good advice, but difficult to follow when this was your first assignment and there was a distinct possibility that you could end up with egg on your face. She had become overconfident, that was her trouble. Tom McNulty was still calling the shots, but it had been her idea to play cat and mouse with Hedley on Friday. "He's been having things too much his own way," she'd said, "so let's move in and make him sweat a little." "With what aim in mind?" McNulty had asked, and she had replied, "To let him know that we're wise to his game and at the same time pull the wool over his eyes. We show him one car and he's so busy watching out for it that he doesn't see the second one. Then maybe we'll get some candid camera shots which could tell us what is really going on." "Brilliant," McNulty had said, "go ahead and do it." And the infrared exposures were the end result, proof that she had the measure of Hedley. Or so she'd thought until a few hours ago.

Right now, however, she had her doubts; right now all she could do was wait for the telephone to break the long silence. When it finally did, she snatched the receiver from the cradle and answered the call with something like a croak.

Kaplin said, "Stop biting your nails, Jan. We're still in the ball game."

"They picked him up at Orly?"

"And tailed him to the Castiglione Hotel on the Rue Faubourg St. Honoré."

"Well, hallelujah."

"I thought you'd be pleased."

"And relieved," she said. "You don't know how relieved. I can't begin to thank you enough."

"You're welcome," Kaplin said modestly. "It's all part of the service."

There was a faint click, followed by a continuous purring noise, and she slowly replaced the phone, her eyes fixed on the montage of photographs on the desk. "You bastard," she said to Hedley. "I'm too young for gray hairs."

The desk clerk had warned Hedley that he had a visitor, and he was there waiting to open the door when the caller pressed the buzzer. The man was short, had dark wiry hair, a sallow complexion, and an immaculate set of teeth which looked as though they'd been capped.

Still wearing a broad smile, he produced his ID card and said, "Monsieur Hedley—my name's Jean-Luc Poirier." His English was good, his accent and tone of voice an accurate impersonation of Maurice Chevalier.

"A good likeness." Hedley opened his passport. "Better than mine."

"I have seen photographs that flattered you more," Poirier said as he moved past him into the bedroom.

"When was this?"

"A week ago."

Hedley snapped his fingers. "In the newspapers."

"Wrong. They were sent over by courier."

Winter: he might have guessed that Winter would have covered all the angles.

"Did you know that our American friends followed you from the airport?"

"No, but I'm glad to hear it." Hedley waved him to a chair and sat down on the bed. "It would have been rather embarrassing if they'd lost me."

"It's a game you're playing?"

"You could say that."

"The rules must be very complicated." Poirier smiled. "Still, that is not my concern. I am just a man who obeys orders."

"You're not the only one."

"We could go on all day like this," said Poirier. "What is it you want from us?"

Hedley lay back on the bed, his hands clasped behind his neck. "I'm on a whirlwind tour of France," he said. "First Reims, then Cannes."

"By road or rail?'

"I'm planning to hire a Renault later this afternoon."

"Is that so?"

"Well, it's more fun traveling by road even though I do occasionally lose my way. That's why I'd like a couple of guides, one in Reims, the other in Cannes."

"Plainclothes?"

"Uniform," said Hedley. "Blue tunic, silver buttons, red stripe down the pants, white gloves, kepi—the whole bag of tricks."

"Now I've heard everything," Poirier said, slapping his forehead.

"Not yet you haven't," said Hedley. "There's a lot more to come."

8.

The moment Hedley turned into the drive and saw the hotel, he knew that La Bouée would have met with Garbo's approval. Way off the beaten track in the pine-covered hills ten miles northwest of Cannes, the small hotel was tailor-made for those who wanted seclusion.

"No need to look any further," he said aloud, and then repeated it in French for the benefit of the gendarme sitting beside him in the Renault.

"We have found the place you are looking for, monsieur?"

"We most certainly have." Hedley switched off the engine. "Now all we have to do is check the hotel register."

"But of course." The gendarme was matter-of-fact as though he understood exactly what was going on, but his furrowed brow gave him away.

"There's really nothing to it," said Hedley. "I just want to ask the proprietor a few questions."

"About a man and a woman involved in a major currency swindle that happened in 1951?"

"That's right." It wasn't much of a cover story, but it was the best he and Poirier could put together in the time available.

"It must be a very important case."

"I'll say it is. The Bank of England lost the equivalent of

2,000 million francs." Hedley got out of the car, waited for the gendarme to join him, and then led the way inside.

According to the Michelin Guide, La Bouée was a comfortable hotel. The symbols denoted that it had fifteen rooms and the food was said to be good for its class but not worth a detour. There was nothing to indicate that the hotel had once been a private villa or that the exterior was pleasing to the eye.

The vestibule was cool and dark, the air heavy with the scent of carnations. The staff were conspicuous by their absence and Hedley was obliged to ring the bell several times before a stout, gray-haired woman emerged from the office to the rear of the reception desk.

The gendarme said, "You are the proprietress, madame?"

"No, I am the concierge." A wisp of hair broke loose from the bun behind her neck and she pushed it back with an impatient flick. "Monsieur Lamont is the owner."

"We'd like to see him, madame."

"He is in Athens on holiday." The concierge drew herself up to her full height and looked the gendarme in the eye. "I am in charge while Monsieur Lamont is away."

"I see." The gendarme mulled it over and then pointed to Hedley. "This gentleman is an English police officer, madame, and he would like to examine your records."

"Would he indeed?" The concierge removed her spectacles and polished the lenses on her apron. Replacing them, she peered at Hedley as if he were an alien from another planet. "Well, I don't know about that. This is a very respectable hotel."

"I know it is." Hedley smiled. "The Prefect of Police in Cannes told me so. He also said that he was quite certain the owners would be only too pleased to help me. I'm sure we can rely on you to do the same."

A little flattery often went a long way and he laid it on with a trowel. He told her that La Bouée was known to be a first-class hotel, that people from all over the world came to stay there, but as with any other well-run establishment, some of the guests were not always what they seemed. Appearances were often deceptive and the couple he was looking for had frequented some of the best hotels in London and Paris.

"And you think these people may have stayed here at La Bouée, monsieur?" she said when he paused for breath.

"We've been told they spent one night here between the eighth and the twenty-fifth of September 1951."

"But that's more than five years ago."

"Yes. Of course I doubt if you would remember them now, but the man was about sixty-one, quite tall, had broad shoulders and thinning hair, and spoke with an American accent. His companion was considerably younger, an attractive-looking English woman—obviously well-bred—dark hair—upturned nose —in her early forties." Hedley opened his wallet and produced a passport photograph for her inspection. "This is the man," he said, "but I'm afraid it's not a very good likeness. He looks rather startled because it was taken shortly after he was arrested."

The photograph had been supplied by Miles Abbott who'd gone through the personnel files looking for a civil servant whose features would seem vaguely familiar but not so familiar that someone would immediately say, "But surely that's General Eisenhower."

"There is something about his face . . . " The concierge broke off frowning, then shook her head. "No, I can't say I remember him."

"Well, I'm not surprised, madame," said Hedley. "After all, five years is a long time to remember a face when you have so many visitors. Perhaps I could see the registration cards for September '51?"

"1951," she repeated. "Ah yes, they will be in the cellar. If monsieur will please excuse me?"

Hedley moved to one side. Raising the counter flap, the concierge stepped past him and waddled across the foyer to open a door under the staircase. Muttering to herself, she switched on the light and descended into the cellar. Five minutes later she reappeared, carrying a loose-leaf binder gray with dust. Using her apron as a duster, she gave the binder a quick wipe before handing it to Hedley.

The registration slips, each the size of an average post-card, were filed in date order. Twelve protruding tabs marked the beginning of each month and it was possible to tell at a glance that with the end of the summer holidays, the number of visitors in September was well down on the total for August. Business had tailed off even more markedly after the second week in September, but he was lucky enough to find a card for Wednesday the eighteenth that met most of the requirements Abbott had stipulated.

"Here we are," Hedley said triumphantly. "Mr. and Mrs. Ralph Stuyvesant of Columbus, Ohio. He's using a different name now but he can't disguise his signature."

He tore the flimsy from the binder, folded it in two, and tucked it into his wallet. The concierge didn't say anything, but from the expectant look in her eyes, it was obvious that she expected a handsome tip. The whirlwind tour of France was costing a small fortune but although Abbott had told him to keep the expenses down, he didn't see how he could give her less than five pounds. Extracting five 1000-franc notes from his wallet, he pressed them into her hand.

"You have been most helpful, madame," he said gravely.

"It has been a pleasure, monsieur," she cooed.

He shook her hand, said, "Au revoir," and walked out into the bright sunlight, the gendarme close on his heels. The last three days had been pretty hectic but now the end was in sight. Provided he could reach the airport in Nice on time, there was a BEA flight to London at 1540 hours, and then all he had to do was mail the registration slip to the usual post office box number.

By 1:45 the canteen was practically deserted; by 1:45 Deakin had finished the stewed prunes and custard and was preparing to enjoy a pipe of tobacco when Bill Turnock approached his table carrying a lunch tray. Unloading a steak and kidney pie, some crackers and cheese, and a cup of dark brown liquid that could have passed for either tea or coffee, he dumped the tray on one of the kitchen trolleys and sat down.

"The things we do for our womenfolk," he grumbled. "Another ten minutes and I'd have to have gone without."

"You have my sympathy, Bill." Deakin looked longingly at his pipe, then deciding that he could hardly smoke it while the other man was eating, put it away in his jacket pocket. "I get caught every Saturday morning when I'm not on duty."

"Caught for what, George?"

"Shopping. Isn't that what you've been doing in the lunch hour?"

"You wouldn't catch me bringing home the groceries." Turnock attacked the steak and kidney pie with a knife and fork, cutting himself a man-sized portion which he ate without relish. "It's Joan's birthday tomorrow," he said between mouthfuls of mashed potato and peas. "Thought I'd take her to the theater."

"Very nice," Deakin said, nodding his head.

"Well, she's been on at me to see *The Mousetrap*."

"I'm told it's very good."

"It must be," Turnock said moodily. "I had to settle for a couple of seats in the circle. The ticket agency told me the play is booked solid for months ahead and I was lucky to get two last-minute cancellations."

"Why all the doom and gloom, then?"

"I'm not really a fan of Agatha Christie; her plots are too convoluted for me."

"Now there we differ," Deakin said amiably. "I like a good mystery."

Turnock stopped eating and looked up. "Talking of mysteries," he said, "I almost bumped into Miles Abbott on the way back. He was just coming out of a stamp shop on St. Martin's Street. When he spotted me, he did a smart about-turn."

"Perhaps he'd forgotten something."

"Rubbish, George. He was determined to avoid me."

Deakin wasn't altogether surprised. Turnock had a positive gift for rubbing people the wrong way, and whenever a suitable opportunity arose he took great delight in scoring points off

Miles Abbott, whose war record with the Special Operations Executive had been somewhat undistinguished. One of the first volunteers to join the French Section, Abbott had had the great misfortune to break both legs in a practice jump when his parachute had failed to open properly. Although fully fit when he was discharged from hospital five months later, Miles had been destined to spend the rest of the war as an instructor with Number 26 Special Training School at Arisaig in the Highlands of Scotland where, of course, he'd never heard a shot fired in anger.

"I'm sure you're wrong, Bill," Deakin said soothingly. "Miles isn't the kind of man to snub anyone; he's far too well-mannered for that."

"You always were a diplomat, George, but I can give you several very good reasons why Abbott should want to avoid me. For one thing, he's been cooking the books."

"You mean the Imprest Account?" Deakin said incredulously.

"What else?" Turnock decided he'd had enough of the steak and kidney pie and moved on to the cheese and crackers. "I was on the quarterly audit yesterday and some of the latest entries looked very peculiar to me. For instance, when we came to reconcile the bank statement for the quarter ending the thirtieth of September, I noticed that the sum of £105 had been paid to the Contingency Fund on the fifth of October. Can you guess what Abbott said when I asked him for an explanation?"

"I haven't the faintest idea, Bill."

" 'A contra entry, old boy.' " Turnock wrinkled his nose in disgust. "He must think I was born yesterday. I tell you, George, he drew that sum in cash and handed it over to Hedley."

"That's a pretty large assumption." Deakin paused. "Or can you prove it?"

"Well, you answer me this, George—what does Hedley earn in a month?"

Deakin scratched his head. The basic salary was £1100 per

annum, but he also recalled that Hedley had been entitled to a local overseas allowance which was worth another £160. Adding the two sums together dividing by twelve, he arrived at an answer that was not wholly to his liking. "He was owed £105 at the end of September," Deakin said slowly.

"Well, there you are then," Turnock crowed. "Abbott put it in his hot little hand the day after he left Burnham House."

"I wonder?"

"I know what you're thinking, George, but I'm not jumping to false conclusions. There were two other transfers: seventy-five pounds on Thursday the ninth and a further seventy-five last Friday. According to Abbott, the commandant of the training wing had overspent his budget and these sums were intended to tide him over until his supplementary estimates are approved by the Finance Committee."

"It's not an unusual arrangement, Bill. As a matter of fact, I was forced to do the same exactly a year ago." Deakin smiled. "Do I sound like the devil's advocate?" he asked.

"Abbott doesn't need one; he's got the paymaster on his side." Turnock finished the last of the cheese and crackers and wiped his mouth on a paper napkin. "I was assured that everything was in order," he continued, "that the Contingency Fund had simply been reimbursed from the Imprest Account for bills that had already been paid on behalf of the training wing."

"And so you signed on the dotted line?"

"I know when I'm fighting a losing battle, George. The odds were two to one against and the paymaster is supposed to be the financial wizard of this establishment. I signed all right, but that doesn't mean I was satisfied with their explanations."

"Are you suggesting that Miles has misappropriated the sum of £255?"

Turnock looked around the canteen and saw that he and Deakin had the place to themselves except for one of the cleaners sweeping the floor near the serving hatch. Moving the dirty plates aside, he leaned forward, resting both elbows on the table.

"Abbott has certainly been dipping into the till," he said,

keeping his voice low, "but I don't think it was his idea. I figure Winter authorized those transactions and told the paymaster to blind me with science."

"I find that very hard to believe," Deakin said quickly.

"Would you believe that Abbott has suddenly acquired another office in the basement?"

"Not unless I saw it for myself."

"I was down there this morning with the chief archivist," Turnock said, unabashed by Deakin's skepticism. "It so happens the Foreign Office wants another club to beat the Americans with, and we were going through some of the dead files relating to King Farouk because I remembered they contained some evidence which proved that the coup d'etat in '52 had been engineered by the CIA. Anyway, I saw Abbott emerge from what used to be a storeroom at the far end of the basement. I admit that I only caught a brief glimpse but, take it from me, that old storeroom has now become a drawing office."

"A drawing office?" Deakin echoed.

"That's right. And he's sharing it with another man, a very reticent man who locked the door behind him."

"Miles is one of the leading lights of our amateur dramatic society. Maybe he's working on their next production."

"During office hours?" Turnock snorted. "Oh, come on, George, you know Abbott is too straight-laced to do a thing like that. Why can't you face the facts and admit it?"

"Admit what?"

"That Winter is running an illegal operation, one that involves Hedley, Abbott, the paymaster, and the unknown recluse in the basement."

"It must be a pretty small-scale affair then," said Deakin. "You can hardly set the world on fire with £255."

"You haven't given it enough thought, George. They can raise whatever capital is necessary whenever they like. Winter is now Deputy Control which means he's also the chairman of the Finance Committee. Since he's already got the paymaster playing in his team, who amongst the remaining committee members is going to oppose him?"

"Well, there is Edmunds, the new Head of Administration, and the Treasury Official."

Deakin paused and thought about it. He could forget Edmunds. He wasn't due to hand over the training wing until the end of the month and he would still be finding his feet when the Finance Committee met on the second of November. The Treasury Official was not a man to be dismissed lightly, but he was only responsible for checking the supplementary estimates. The actual bookkeeping and the subsequent distribution of funds to the various departments was in the hands of the paymaster, a man who was very adept at juggling the figures.

"I've changed my mind," said Deakin. "Winter can do pretty much as he likes."

"So what are we going to do about it?"

"I'm not cut out to be a crusader, Bill."

"What do you mean by that?" Turnock found it difficult to keep his voice down.

"In plain English it means I don't want to be involved. You signed the audit proceedings, not me. If you want to take this matter up with the head man, that's your prerogative, but in my view, you'll only be making a fool of yourself. Let's face it, Bill, you haven't got a shred of proof." Deakin pushed back his chair. "It's time we were moving," he said. "The cleaners want to get on with their job and I have work to do."

"Wait a minute." Turnock reached across the table and grabbed him by the wrist. "What if I managed to produce a really solid bit of evidence? Would you support me then?"

"I think I'd consider holding your hand, Bill."

"Thanks, George." Turnock released his wrist and smiled. "That's all I wanted to know."

Janet Roscoe put the phone down and slowly counted up to ten. Still angry, she vented her temper on the typewriter, hitting the keys with such venomous force that each letter left a deep indentation in the sheet of foolscap. Her lips mouthing the words, she typed up the brief message Kaplin had phoned in, and then, pulling the release lever back, snatched the report from the carriage and offered it to Tom McNulty who was standing beside her.

"You read it, Jan," he said. "I'll absorb it better that way."

"Okay, Tom. It says, quote: BEA flight from Nice arrived Heathrow 1710 hours. Subject passed through Customs ten minutes later, entered main concourse, and stopped by mailbox to post a letter before taking cab to Gresham Square."

"Good. Now let's go back to the beginning."

"What?"

"I want to be sure of all the facts." McNulty reached past her and opened the folder lying on the desk near the typewriter. "Monday the fifteenth of October," he said, indicating the appropriate paragraph, "Hedley arrives Paris, checks into Castiglione Hotel. Take it from there and give it to me in your own words, not this official jargon. The guy has got a name, so let's use it instead of referring to him as the subject."

"I prefer subject," she said. "It's impersonal."

"Maybe so, but it doesn't help you to be objective about Hedley. He still gets under your skin."

Much as Janet hated to admit it, she knew Tom was right. Hedley was deliberately taunting them, but it was stupid to over-react just because he was making everybody jump through the hoop.

"He won't in future," she said grimly. "That's a promise."

McNulty smiled. "When you're ready, Jan," he said.

"Right." Janet glanced at the paragraph McNulty had indicated earlier and quickly assimilating all the facts, said, "Shortly after checking into the hotel, Hedley was visited by Jean-Luc Poirier from the Police Judiciaire on the Quai des Orfèvres. They talked for just over an hour and then, some ten minutes after Poirier had departed, Hedley also left the hotel on foot and made his way to a rental agency in the Ninth Arrondissement where he arranged to hire a car. Early the following morning, he returned to the garage, collected the Renault, and drove back to the hotel to pick up his overnight bag."

Leaving Paris on Route Nationale 2, Hedley had made his way via Soissons to Reims and the central police station in the

88

Place Carnegie. Accompanied by a gendarme, he had subsequently visited the Univers Hotel on the Boulevard Foch, The Crystal in the Place d'Erlon, and a secluded villa twelve miles out of town on the road to Montcornet. Returning to Reims late in the afternoon, he had dropped the gendarme at the station and headed south, driving as far as Chalon where he'd stayed the night. On Wednesday morning he'd set off from Chalon at 8:30 and continued southward through Lyon, Valence, Avignon, Aix-en-Provence, and on to Cannes. There he had met the Prefect of Police before checking into the Château de la Tour. Thursday morning had seen a repeat performance of the Reims episode, with Hedley visiting several out-of-the-way hotels northwest of Cannes before ending up at La Bouée.

"He saw the concierge, told her he was an English police officer investigating a massive currency swindle which dated back to 1951, and asked to see the hotel register for that year. Since the gendarme supported his story, the concierge had no reason to disbelieve him and as a result Hedley removed a registration slip made out by a Mr. Stuyvesant of Columbus, Ohio. He then left La Bouée and after dropping the gendarme off in Cannes, went on to Nice where he returned the Renault to the rental agency before catching the BEA flight to London. The rest you know."

"Reims." McNulty grunted. "Eisenhower established his headquarters there toward the end of the war. Summersby was a lieutenant in the WACs by that time, but hell, that's ancient history and there's no mileage in it for Winter. If the smear campaign is to work, he had to prove that the old love affair was given a new lease on life when Eisenhower was Supreme Commander of NATO. I guess Winter avoided Versailles because it was too close to NATO Headquarters and nobody would believe that Ike would be crass enough to mess his own doorstep. The trip to Reims was just a buildup for Cannes."

"Is there any chance the registration slip is genuine, Tom? I mean, could Eisenhower have spent a night at La Bouée with Kay Summersby?"

"No, no, it's a frame-up. I did some checking with the

Pentagon, and according to their records this Major Rupert Flaxman of Wyecroft Farm was a member of Eisenhower's personal staff from '50 to '52. I've no idea how Winter got on to it but it seems Flaxman was responsible for scheduling Ike's appointments and I'm betting he held on to those diaries after he left the army. It would explain why Hedley went to see him and what was in that brown paper parcel he was carrying when Kaplin photographed him outside the Underground station in Sloane Square. The way I see it, Abbott went through those diaries looking for a date that would stand up and when he found one, Hedley was sent over to France to collect the necessary material. There are some pretty good forgers in the ranks of the SIS. By the time they've finished doctoring the registration ship, even Ike will believe he signed the goddamned thing."

"I guess they'll also produce a number of letters to show that he's kept in touch with Kay Summersby over the years."

"Sure they will," said McNulty. "A whole bundle of them. But the registration slip is the real clincher. It proves Ike finally made it with her."

"Then we missed a great opportunity to throw a monkey wrench into the works." Janet reached for the packet of Chesterfields on the desk and lit a cigarette. "Kaplin wanted to bounce Hedley when he arrived at Heathrow."

"We've been over that ground before," McNulty said wearily.

They had argued the pros and cons all afternoon, but nothing she could say would make Tom change his mind, and he'd insisted they play it his way. She still thought he was wrong.

"The Paris office warned us he was on the 1540 flight from Nice and we had more than two hours to set it up. Kaplin said he could have picked Hedley clean without him knowing a thing about it. We should have given him the green light he was asking for."

"Kaplin is an optimist." McNulty moved around the desk and helped himself to one of Janet's cigarettes. "Suppose Hedley felt Kaplin's hand dip into his pocket and socked him one? Next thing we know, our man is up in court and we've got egg on our faces." He shook his head vehemently. "No, we handle this situation my way and play it cool."

"For how long?" she asked.

"Until Winter makes the first positive move. Up to now he's been pussyfooting around. He's saying to us, 'Look what I'm collecting on Eisenhower; if he doesn't accommodate us over Suez, I'm going to throw the shit into the fan.' "

"So?"

"So we call his bluff and do nothing. That way we force his hand and he has to come out into the open." McNulty lit the cigarette and inhaled deeply. "It's a question of timing," he said. "The British and the French aren't ready to go to war yet. The RAF has only just begun to fly their *Valiant* jet bombers out to Malta."

"I didn't know that, Tom," she said, frowning at her cigarette.

"We've been keeping a discreet watch on their airfields. The first squadron departed last night. Third Air Force decided to exercise the airborne early warning system and our planes tracked them right across Europe."

There had been other indications that things were heating up. The Sixth Fleet had intercepted a message to H.M.S. *Newcastle*, ordering the cruiser, which was in the Indian Ocean bound for Australia, to escort the Duke of Edinburgh on the next stage of his world tour, to turn about and proceed to Port Sudan with utmost despatch. French army units assembled in the Marseilles-Toulon area were starting to embark on troop transports, and one CIA agent had managed to procure a bundle of currency overprinted Occupation of Egypt.

"The British are also having trouble on the home front," he continued. "Some of Eden's cabinet aren't too happy about his policy. Sir Walter Monckton resigned as Minister of Defense today."

"I know," said Janet. "I read the newspapers too. They said it was for reasons of health."

"Yeah. Well, now it looks as though the hawks in Eden's cabinet are in the ascendancy and, taking the state of their military preparations into account, I'd say the curtain will go up around the thirtieth of October. Eisenhower's re-election campaign will be entering the final days and that would be a good time for Winter to move in and lean on him." McNulty spread his hands. "Of course I'm only thinking out loud, but he could tell Hedley to give the dirt to some scandal sheet."

"Or to one of the American press correspondents in London?" Janet suggested.

"Unlikely, wouldn't you say?" McNulty frowned, then suddenly snapped his fingers. "Hell no—Winter can't afford to do anything this side of the pond. He's running an illegal operation."

"That's crazy."

"You think so? Look, if this is aboveboard, why didn't he arrange for someone to meet Hedley at Heathrow? Why leave him to mail the registration slip? Jesus Christ, when Hedley was kicked out of Budapest, Winter used all of his resources to smuggle him out of the airport and away to Burnham House. He couldn't do the same thing this evening because he has to run this operation on a shoestring. Don't you see? The more people he involves, the greater the risk of exposure. Hedley and Abbott, they're the only guys he's got on his team."

"I think you're wrong, Tom." Janet stubbed out her cigarette. "I believe Winter does have official backing, otherwise I can't see how he could ask Poirier and the Police Judiciaire for help."

"Winter probably told Poirier he had government approval. Not that the French could care less one way or the other—they want this war more than the British do. An illegal operation," McNulty smiled and shook his head. "Jesus, that's beautiful."

"Is it?"

"Sure it is; it means we've got Winter over a barrel. Like I said, he can't do anything this side of the pond. He's got to send Hedley stateside."

"Why not Abbott?"

"He's not a field agent."

"I see." Janet brushed her skirt, removing the ash that had

92

fallen onto it. "So what do we do, Tom? Cancel Hedley's visa on the grounds that he's an undesirable alien?"

"And show our hand? No, we let him go to New York, and that will be the moment you've been waiting for."

"The moment I've been waiting for?" she echoed in a small voice.

"To play dirty," said McNulty.

9.

Deakin cracked the shell, laid the teaspoon aside, picked up a knife and with the dexterity of a surgeon neatly sliced the top off his boiled egg. The white and the raw yolk fused together and the overspill ran down the side of the egg-cup on to the plate, where it formed a small congealing pool. There was nothing he enjoyed more for breakfast than two lightly boiled eggs but the gooey mess in front of him took the edge off his appetite and made him feel queasy.

"Are the eggs not to your liking, George?" Marjorie inquired anxiously.

Deakin looked up with a sickly smile. "They're fine, dear," he assured her.

"That one looks very runny to me." Marjorie frowned. "I don't understand it," she said. "I boiled them for three minutes."

Her eyes instinctively went to the refrigerator and he knew that she had forgotten to leave the carton out overnight. The water had undoubtedly gone off the boil the moment she placed the eggs in the saucepan, but if he pointed this out to Marjorie, it would only upset her.

"Is Coral not up yet?" he said, changing the subject.

"It's Saturday, George."

"Yes, I know. Unfortunately, I have to go into the office."

"It's getting to be a habit."

Her voice was neutral but the innuendo was clear enough. He was using pressure of work as an excuse to avoid the weekly shopping expedition.

"We are very busy, dear," he said mildly.

"Yes, so you keep telling me." Marjorie pouted, a sign which told him that she was about to pursue the matter, but then the letter box rattled out in the hall and she forgot what she was going to say. "That will be the paper boy," she muttered.

"I expect so," Deakin said, buttering a slice of toast.

Marjorie sighed, turned the gas down under the kettle, and left the kitchen. From the foot of the staircase she called to Coral that breakfast was on the table; from the landing above her daughter snapped that she would be down in a minute. Listening to the exchange, Deakin hoped she wouldn't hurry herself; a little of Coral went a very long way and he could do without her company over breakfast.

"I was wrong, George. It was the postman." Slowly, as if still half asleep, Marjorie returned to the kitchen and placed a small white envelope on the table. "I wonder who it's from?" she said. "I don't recognize the writing."

Deakin glanced at the envelope. "Neither do I."

"Aren't you going to open it?"

"My hands are sticky," he said. "Besides, it's addressed to you."

"So it is." Marjorie picked up the envelope again, opened the flap, and extracted a card. "Some people called Squires have invited us to dinner on Wednesday the twenty-fourth of October." Her eyebrows met in a puzzled frown. "Do we know them, George?"

"Alan Squires is an old friend of mine."

"Really? I don't remember you mentioning his name before."

"I used to see quite a lot of him when I was with the British Middle East Office but we lost touch after I was posted home in October 1950. Alan was working for the government of Bahrain in those days and, in a funny kind of way, I suppose he's still looking after their commercial interests." Deakin helped himself to another slice of toast. "He's with the Crown Agents now and their head office is in Millbank. I happened to bump into him the other day when I was taking a lunchtime stroll along the Embankment."

"And that was the first time you'd seen him in how long?"

"Very nearly seven years."

"Good heavens." Marjorie warmed the teapot, measured four spoonfuls from the caddy, and then filled the teapot with boiling water. "Still, they do say it's a small world."

"Yes, well, it'll be nice to see Alan and June again." Deakin heard Coral's heavy footsteps on the stairs and quickly added, "You'd like to go, wouldn't you, Marjorie?"

"Next Wednesday? It's rather short notice, isn't it?"

"I'm afraid that's my fault; I forgot to tell you when Alan first asked me." Deakin jabbed a finger at the invitation card. "This is just an *aide-mémoire*; it says so right here at the bottom."

"Oh really, George, you are too bad."

With a sense of timing few actresses could have surpassed, Coral flounced into the kitchen and sat down at the table. Observing the smirk on her narrow, spiteful face, Deakin guessed that she had overheard the conversation.

"Don't tell me you two are quarreling again," she said, filling a bowl with cornflakes.

Deakin ignored the jibe, a passive form of resistance which, although wholly negative, was infinitely preferable to an all-out war of attrition. He had been aware of Coral's hostility from that very first night in Zermatt, almost six long years ago, when the headwaiter had showed him to their table; but as his friendship with Marjorie began to develop into something much more he had chosen to turn a blind eye. "Give her time," Marjorie had pleaded, "and she will come to like you. Coral is only sixteen and she was terribly fond of her father." They were two lonely people and he had wanted to believe Marjorie and in the first two years of their marriage he had gone out of his way to win Coral's approval. He had tried kindness, affection,

96

appeasement, and firmness, all to no avail. The harder he tried to build a bridge the wider the gulf became between them and, in the end he'd given it up as a bad job. He had persuaded himself that Coral was not unattractive, that one day she was bound to get married, but as yet there was no sign of a steady boyfriend and lately he had begun to wonder if one would ever materialize. At sixteen, Coral had merely been a jealous, thoroughly spoiled teenager; at twenty-two, she was an opinionated, vindictive, nasty-tempered shrew.

"It'll make a nice change for you, Marjorie," he said, picking up from where they'd left off. "We hardly ever go out."

"And whose fault is that?" Coral demanded.

For a few heady seconds, Deakin cherished a wild impulse to push her face into the bowl of cornflakes. Exercising all his self-control, he said, "I realize I shouldn't have accepted Alan's invitation without consulting you first, Marjorie, but he wouldn't take no for an answer." To his own ears, he sounded pathetic, like a small boy begging his mother for forgiveness, but he wanted to have dinner with Alan and June and he wanted Marjorie to go with him.

"There's no need to apologize, George." Marjorie smiled. "I'll gladly come with you."

"Oh good, I know you'll like them." His relief was such that Deakin felt he had to show his gratitude in some way. "Perhaps we could do the shopping this afternoon?" he suggested. "With any luck, I should be home by 12:30."

"Well, that's very thoughtful of you, George, but I'm sure Coral will help me."

"Sorry, I can't." Coral tossed her head, a mannerism Deakin found particularly irritating. "I'm supporting a protest demonstration in London. We intend to picket the War Office."

The War Office was too close to Broadway for comfort and Deakin just hoped that Coral and her motley crew of friends wouldn't take it into their heads to pay them a visit. He wondered how Winter would react should they happen to turn up on the doorstep with their banners. Knowing Charles, he might well persuade one of the cleaners to empty a bucket of cold water over their heads. A mental picture of a bedraggled Coral arriving home soaked to the skin and with her hair in rats' tails brought a happy smile to his face.

"I don't happen to find it amusing, George."

"What?"

"Eden's policy," Coral snapped. "We want peace, not war."

"Don't we all," said Deakin.

The penman was an ex-RAF bomber pilot who had learned his tradecraft in a prisoner of war camp. A trainee draftsman in peacetime, he had been co-opted by the escape committee and put to work altering the destination and date on old train tickets which the "scroungers" had managed to obtain from their guards by means of bribery and corruption. From this humble beginning he had graduated to identity cards, leave passes, and travel documents which proved good enough to fool the eagle eyes of the Gestapo. In due course, samples of his handiwork had come to the notice of MI9, a wartime organization responsible for assisting the various escape lines established by Resistance workers in occupied Europe and as a result, note had been taken of his talents for future reference.

Like a good many ex-servicemen, the penman had found it extremely difficult to settle down to a humdrum job after the war, and craving something more exciting than a nine-to-five routine for the rest of his life, he had been a natural candidate for the SIS whose recruiting agents had followed his career in civilian life with interest. In Stalag Luft 17, he had achieved remarkable results with the crude and rudimentary materials at his disposal; at Broadway, provided with the finest equipment that money could buy, he had become a supreme artist at his trade. Long an admirer of his work, Winter thought the Eisenhower letters were the best work of their kind that he had ever produced.

"Brilliant," said Winter, "that's the only way to describe them."

Abbott nodded. "He certainly went to enormous trouble to get the texture of the paper and ink exactly right. I'm assured the letters can't be faulted, but he had problems with the registration slip from the hotel La Bouée. Stuyvesant used a ballpoint pen to print his name and address and he was pretty heavy-handed about it. Maybe the ink wasn't flowing properly but, whatever the reason he damn near went through the paper. We had to iron the reverse side to remove the indentations before we could erase his name and signature and make the substitution."

The problem hadn't ended there. Although they had managed to acquire a number of speeches and Orders of the Day that Eisenhower had drafted during the war in his own hand, they had been unable to turn up a single memo or operational map with his comments in block capitals.

"We came to the conclusion that Eisenhower would try to disguise his handwriting," said Abbott. "It's the sort of thing most people would do in the circumstances."

"Quite," said Winter.

"The trouble is, Eisenhower's face is too well known. I mean, who is seriously going to believe that a man in his position would keep an assignation with Kay Summersby in a hotel? In his shoes, I'd ask a close friend if I could use his place."

"La Bouée is a small hotel in the middle of nowhere." Winter smiled. "Going there would be more discreet than staying in a friend's apartment, especially as we picked a date in the off-season."

Eisenhower and Kay Summersby could deny it for all they were worth, but it wouldn't do them any good. At his request, Poirier had already removed the duplicate registration slip from the archives in the Panthéon which meant that, as far as the French police were concerned, the Stuyvesants had never stayed at La Bouée on the eighteenth of September 1951. On the other hand, the SIS could produce a registration form made out by a certain Mr. Ralph Summercorn whose signature bore a strong resemblance to Eisenhower's.

"Summercorn." Winter looked up. "What made you choose that name?"

"A spot of psychology," said Abbott. "Obviously, Eisenhower

would have used an alias, but we decided he'd be too intelligent to pick one that began with the same initial letter. So he started to use hers, then halfway through Summersby he saw the gaffe and hurriedly changed it to Summercorn. At least, that's the impression we tried to create."

"And suceeded."

"Thanks." Abbott hesitated, uncertain how to put the question that was uppermost in his mind. "We've completed the spadework . . . ," he said diffidently.

"So what happens now?" Winter finished the sentence for him. "Well, that's easy. We sit back and wait." Despite Monckton's resignation from the cabinet, despite the fact that the hawks were in the ascendancy, Bracecourt still believed that Eden would draw back from the brink. "In the meantime, I'll hang on to these letters, Miles."

"That's a relief. Now perhaps I can open the safe in my office without having to look over my shoulder to make sure no one is watching."

"Are you telling me that someone has been spying on you?" Winter asked sharply.

"I'm not sure." Abbott shifted his weight from one foot to the other. Although he disliked the idea of snitching on one of his colleagues, he told himself that there was such a thing as a misplaced sense of loyalty. "I'm afraid Bill Turnock gave me a hard time over the Imprest Account. He asked a lot of awkward questions."

"But he signed on the dotted line."

"Only under duress. I don't think he entirely believed our explanations."

"The paymaster thought he did."

"Well, he's entitled to his opinion, but I've a nasty feeling that Turnock knows we've been using one of the storerooms in the basement. He was down there, going through the dead files in the Mideast section with the chief archivist and I'm pretty sure he saw me leaving the drawing office."

"When was this, Miles?"

"The day after the audit. We almost bumped into one another again during the lunch break that same day. I was coming out of the stamp shop on St. Martin's Street when I spotted Turnock on Charing Cross Road, heading toward Trafalgar Square." Abbott shrugged his shoulders. "Perhaps I'm making a mountain out of a molehill. After all, it could have been a coincidence."

Winter hoped he was right but it was a fact that, apart from one minor blemish on his record, Turnock had been a damned good Special Branch officer when he was with the Palestine police force. For a man of his experience and background, shadowing Abbott would have been child's play. True, Miles had eventually spotted him, but that could have been a deliberate error on his part in order to allay suspicion.

"I don't think Bill will give us any trouble, but we'll play it safe just the same. You'd better tell the penman to make himself scarce for a week or two, and then you clear his stuff out of the storeroom."

"Right." Abbott became visibly brighter. "I'll do it this afternoon after everyone has gone."

Winter scowled. It was possible they were closing the stable door after the horse had bolted, but until Turnock made a move, there was little else he could do apart from insuring that Miles stayed out of the limelight until he was ready to send him to New York.

"I want you to telephone Hedley," he said crisply. "Tell him that I'll be contacting him from now on."

"I see." It was evident from his tone of voice that he didn't.

"It's just a safeguard," Winter assured him. "Turnock might take it into his head to follow you and we don't want him to see you and Hedley together." He didn't want Turnock to see Abbott at the bank either. In the future, Miles would have to authorize him to draw whatever cash was necessary from the Imprest Account. A telephone call to the manager in Lombard Street followed by confirmation in writing should do the trick, but that was something they could discuss later. Right now he had other things on his mind, matters he couldn't attend to while Abbott was hovering in front of his desk. "Well now," he said, stretching a hand toward the telephone, "unless there are any questions you want to ask me . . . "

"I can't think of any."

Winter thought it typical of Abbott that he wasn't the least bit offended by the abrupt dismissal. Accorded the same treatment, he knew that Turnock would have been surly while Deakin would have found it difficult to hide his resentment. Reliable, conscientious, unfailingly cheerful—these were just a few of the adjectives that readily sprang to mind whenever he had to write Abbott's confidential report.

Lifting the phone, he rang Leconfield House and asked the girl on the switchboard to put him through to Cleaver's extension. "I have two questions," Winter said after they had gone to secure speech.

"Let me guess," said Cleaver. "First of all, you want to raise the matter of our surveillance on the Egyptian Embassy in South Audley Street, right?"

"You must be clairvoyant."

"Not really," said Cleaver. "By my reckoning, you should have received yesterday's log a couple of hours ago. What's the problem?"

"There are too many unidentified visitors." Winter lifted a folder from the pending tray and flipped it open. "For instance, what's the use of telling me that 'a tall, swarthy-looking man, wearing a blue pinstripe and carrying a rolled umbrella and briefcase, arrived at 10:52 and departed again at 11:48'? We want names, for God's sake, not descriptions. And what the hell happened to those photographs Special Branch were supposed to be taking?"

"I think somebody got out of bed the wrong side this morning."

Other people had said it to him before, but never Cleaver, and the pointed observation brought him up with a nasty jolt. Reluctantly, Winter was forced to recognize that Malcolm Cleaver was right. He had lost his temper for no good reason, a sign that he was beginning to feel the strain. He suspected it was the culmination of many separate factors: the illegal operation with all its attendant risks and the knowledge that Bracecourt would be the first to disown him if anything went wrong. Too many problems were raising their heads at the same time; Bill Turnock acting cussed about the Imprest Account, which was an unpleasant surprise, and the oddly disturbing telephone call from Katherine Lang earlier that morning. Her voice had sounded very brittle, her reasons so unconvincing that he had been hard-pressed to explain to Geraldine why she had asked him to call round on his way home from the office.

"I'm sorry, Malcolm," Winter said contritely. "I'm going through a bad patch. Losing my temper with you was inexcusable."

"Forget it," said Cleaver. "We all have our troubles. Identifying all the people who call at the Egyptian Embassy is no easy task. If the Special Branch officers don't know them by sight they have to make discreet inquiries, and that takes time. As for the photographs, well, I'm afraid we need them to jog a few memories."

"You've just answered my first question."

"Good," said Cleaver. "You needn't bother to raise the other one. Your potential black sheep are behaving themselves like the good little civil servants they are. You'll hear from me the moment one of them puts a foot wrong."

"Thanks."

"So stop worrying—go home—relax—play a round of golf or something."

A round of golf? Cleaver wasn't in a position to appreciate the irony of his suggestion, but Katherine had phoned him shortly after Harry had left for Bushey Park; by now her husband would be approaching the ninth hole.

"Is that what you're about to do?" he asked.

"Of course. What do you think?"

Winter said, "I think you're one hell of a fibber, Malcolm," and heard the other man laugh as he put the phone down.

Carefully gathering the Eisenhower letters together, Winter placed them in the safe and then left the office. It was a fine, bright, October morning, but the warm sun on his back did not lift his spirits. In a somber mood, he set off for Wellington Barracks where his Jaguar was parked by kind permission of the Commanding Officer of the Second Coldstream Guards.

The Langs had chosen to live in Clifton Avenue for widely disparate reasons: Katherine, because she had fallen in love with the elegant, regency-style terraced house at first sight, and Harry, because, metaphorically speaking, Lords was just around the corner and he was a life member of the Marylebone Cricket Club. The close proximity of Regents Park and the London Zoo were two bonus points that hadn't occurred to either of them until Katherine gave birth to their first child eighteen months after moving into Number 38.

A frequent visitor to their house, Winter had often been obliged to drive up and down the avenue looking for somewhere to park, but not this time. Neatly slotting the Jaguar into the vacant space at the curbside which was usually occupied by Harry's Daimler, he got out of the car, walked up the short flight of steps to the house, and rang the bell. A sallow Portuguese girl opened the door and showed him into the drawing room, where Katherine was waiting for him.

"Charles." She came toward him and seized his hands. "How nice to see you," she said.

Discreet as always, she allowed him no more than a friendly peck on one cheek. It was understood the passionate embrace would come later when they were alone, but as the maid closed the door behind her Katherine avoided his arms and walked away.

"I need another drink," she said.

"Another?" Winter raised his eyebrows. "That sounds rather ominous."

"It is." She poured herself a large whiskey from a decanter and then turned to face him once more. "You see, I'm pregnant."

Pregnant? Was it possible? They had been damned careful to prevent this very thing from happening. So why was she so certain that Harry wasn't the father? She must have got it wrong, that was the only explanation.

"Are you sure?" he asked in a hollow voice which sounded a long way off.

"For God's sake, I've missed two months."

The school holidays, he thought. It must have happened in August when the Langs were staying at Bembridge. Harry was a keen sailor and they always rented a cottage by the sea for the month. Katherine had come up to town for the day on some pretext and he had met her for lunch. He recalled it had been a very hot day and Katherine had decided she wanted to take a shower before catching the train back to Portsmouth, and after she had accepted his offer of a lift to Clifton Avenue, they had gone to bed, both of them knowing that this was what they'd intended to do all along.

"I know what you're thinking, Charles, but it's not the menopause. Strange as it may seem to you, a woman can still conceive at forty."

"You do me an injustice." Winter looked her in the eye. "Such a thought never entered my head." But it had, along with others which he could no longer keep to himself. "Have you told Harry yet?" he said, feeling his way along a difficult path like a blind man.

Katherine stared at him for several moments and then burst into laughter. "My God," she spluttered. "How absolutely priceless." The laughter died as suddenly as it had erupted. "Shall I tell you something, Charles? I can't remember when Harry last made love to me."

It took some time for the full import to sink in. When it finally did, he realized there was no room for maneuver and no easy solution. Katherine, Harry, Geraldine, the children—he would hurt them all whatever decision he made.

"We'll see it through together." Winter licked his lips. "I'll talk to Geraldine today."

"And ask her for a divorce?"

"Yes."

"What kind of salary do you get, Charles?"

"What?"

"I said, how much do you earn? It's a simple enough question, isn't it?" Her voice was cold, like an icy wind.

"£3250," he said. "I've just been promoted."

"£3250. I have three children away at boarding school and you have two. Need I say more?"

So this is what it comes to, he thought. *We balance our love for each other against pounds, shillings, and pence.* "We'll manage somehow," he said aloud.

Katherine shook her head. "We're too old to start again. Can you really see either of us as newlyweds, pinching and scraping, watching every penny we spend?"

"Can you think of a better solution?" he countered.

"I already have." Katherine swallowed her whiskey and put the empty glass down. "Harry is off on another business trip at the end of the month. He'll be away for ten days. Plenty of time for me to have an abortion."

"You're mad. I won't hear of it."

"I'll be up and about again before the children come home for half term."

"For Christ's sake," said Winter. "Will you please listen to me for a minute?"

"I've made up my mind, Charles. I've been given the address of a private clinic, but I need 300 guineas and I can hardly ask Harry for it."

The tears welled in her eyes and began to run down both cheeks. He moved toward Katherine and folded his arms about her. He told her that she mustn't worry, that everything would come right for them in the end, but a gut feeling told him that things could never be the same between them again. And he knew too that in tacitly agreeing to an abortion, he had betrayed Katherine and would spend the rest of his life regretting it.

Turnock watched the clock move on to 1:30 and decided it was time he left the pub on Victoria Street. Broadway would be empty by now and he would have the place to himself, except for the duty officers whom he could easily avoid. The War

Department constable on the reception desk might think it odd that he should return to the office on a Saturday afternoon, but he had a perfect excuse ready. If the necessity arose he would simply say he'd suddenly had an awful feeling that he hadn't spun the dial after closing the safe. As a department head he couldn't afford to be lax about security and the constable would certainly believe him when he said he wouldn't have a moment's peace until he made sure the safe was locked.

If the necessity arose? Turnock frowned. Why not come straight out with it? Christ, if he chatted the constable up, he might even get into the building without signing in. Ten minutes, that's all he needed to break into the storeroom in the basement and obtain enough evidence to convince Deakin and make him climb down off the fence.

So, all right, he was going to arrive home late and there would be hell to pay from Joan, but that was a small price to pay. In any case, she would soon come around when he waved the invitation for Wednesday the twenty-fourth of October under her nose. No matter what Joan had to say about it, his job did have some perks, like this invitation to dinner from Sven Uddenberg, the Middle East Airlines representative in London. "You're in charge of the Arabian desk now," Deakin had explained. "That's why our Swedish friend invited you. It's a once-a-year thing but the food's good and it's worth going for that alone, never mind what you might learn from him."

Turning the corner into Broadway, Turnock quickened his stride, yesterday's Special Branch officer about to put his whole future at risk for no reason other than he hated a girl named Esther Rabinowitz and distrusted Winter.

10.

The duty officers had spent a busy Sunday decoding a spate of telegrams from Budapest and Warsaw. None had been so urgent that Deakin had been obliged to go into the office, but the resident clerk had telephoned his home several times to give him the general picture. As a result, he arrived early at the office on Monday morning, knowing there had been some very interesting developments in Hungary and Poland over the weekend.

Deakin began the morning with the batch of cables from the Head of Station, Warsaw, believing that the dramatic events in Poland could well have a bearing on the explosive situation in Hungary. The Poznan riots in July had been a spontaneous protest against working conditions but they had also sparked off a major reappraisal of party doctrine. So long as the Polish Communist Party observed the guidelines laid down at the Twentieth Party Congress, the Kremlin had had no cause for alarm, but in recent weeks Polish nationalism had begun to rear its head and that was something that did worry Khrushchev. If left unchecked, nationalism could seriously undermine the ties with the Soviet Union, a distinct possibility since, unlike the Hungarian government, the Stalinist hard-liners in the Polish Communist Party were heavily outnumbered. Unfortunately for Khrushchev, when the Kremlin had tried to intervene, the SB secret police had refused to support the hard-liners and the Internal Security forces had held Rokossowski's troops in check.

That much was history. On Saturday, Khrushchev, Kaganovitch, Mikoyan, and Molotov had arrived unannounced in Warsaw, only to find that the majority of the Central Committee and the Polish government were aligned against them. The next day, October 21, Gomulka had been elected First Secretary of the Party with the enforced approval of the Soviet leaders. The head of the SIS station in Warsaw had also reported that the Red Army units marching in support of the Soviet delegation had been ordered to withdraw to their bases. The report was graded B2, meaning the source was usually reliable and the information could be valid. Although only time would tell whether there was any substance to the report, Deakin felt optimistic enough to attach a note to the folder predicting that the Soviets had just suffered a major diplomatic reverse, one which could have profound effects elsewhere.

The cables from Budapest were equally significant. A list of demands, similar to those produced by Judit and Zoltan Mikes in their manifesto, had been widely distributed by the influential writers' association and, in Gerö's absence on an official visit to Yugoslavia, the engineering students had organized a vast meeting at the Polytechnic on Sunday which had unanimously called for far-reaching reforms. Toby Johnston, the resident SIS man, had also learned that a massive demonstration was being planned for Tuesday the twenty-third of October, and, last but not least, three provincial units, the Thirty-seventh Infantry, First Motorized, and the Thirty-third Tank Regiments had been placed on full alert in case they were needed to reinforce the Budapest garrison.

Deakin read the Budapest cables again, making brief notes for Winter's benefit as he went along. "There is," he wrote, "reason to feel gratified on two counts. Firstly, Toby Johnston has obviously managed to repair the damage caused by Hedley's sudden expulsion from Hungary and the information is beginning to flow again; and secondly, our assessment of the situation is being vindicated daily. Matters could well come to a head on Tuesday but much will depend on the attitude of the Hungarian Army." Deakin paused, then, recalling what he'd heard about the state of morale in the Hungarian armed forces, began to repeat his comments. Completely engrossed in what he was doing, it took more than Turnock's tap on the door to disturb his concentration.

"Can you spare me a few minutes, George?"

Deakin looked up frowning and only managed a halfhearted smile when he saw who it was. "Is it important, Bill?"

"I happen to think so." Turnock closed the door behind him. "You see, we've just heard that the Israelis are planning to mobilize on the twenty-fifth."

"Where did that rumor come from?"

"Our friends across the Channel—and it's no rumor."

"How very interesting."

"Come off it, George, you're beginning to sound like Winter." Turnock pulled up a chair and sat down. "You know damn well that they'll be able to launch a major offensive five days later. They will destroy the Egyptian Army in the Sinai and march on the Suez Canal, and then we'll go in, ostensibly to separate the belligerents."

"It's a plausible hypothesis, Bill," Deakin said patiently, "one that you and I have expounded at some length. However, as Winter pointed out to us at the time, it's based on a misconception. Whatever the French may think, the pro-Israel lobby in the United States isn't weighty enough to have any real influence on their presidential election. Rest assured, the Foreign Office will have already told Eden that Dulles will be down on us like a ton of bricks if we lift a finger against Nasser."

"Dulles is not the president; Eisenhower is, and Winter plans to take care of him."

"Ah yes, the Imprest Account." Deakin heaved a deep sigh. "Don't tell me I'm about to hear another episode of that enthralling saga?"

"You can sneer as much as you like, George, but it's no

joking matter. You weren't in the office on Saturday afternoon."

Turnock was noted for his thin skin and quick temper. Should anyone be unwise enough to cross swords with him, he usually reacted like a bull on the rampage. For him to remain placid when his pet theory was being subjected to ridicule was something of a revelation to Deakin.

"You didn't see the moving man in action," he added.

"What are you talking about?"

"I'm talking about Miles Abbott," said Turnock. "He found himself a part-time job shifting furniture."

"The storeroom in the basement?"

"Right. It's back to what it was before Winter commandeered it."

Turnock had spent some minutes chatting to the War Department constable on duty in the main entrance of 54 Broadway and had then taken the lift up to the fourth floor, supposedly to make sure his office safe was locked. The section duty officer had been listening to the sports commentary on the radio and, stealing past his room, Turnock had opened the door to the internal fire escape and made his way down to the basement. Provided everything went according to plan, Turnock had figured he could pick the mortice lock, check out the storeroom, and retrace his steps to the main entrance inside ten minutes.

"The best-laid plans have a habit of going astray," Turnock said ruefully. "I damn near came face to face with Abbott. Luckily, he had his back to me and was dragging a raised workbench, the kind of thing architects use. Anyway, I had to duck behind a concrete pillar to avoid him as he went out to the stairwell. As soon as it was safe to move, I found myself a better hiding place behind the filing racks at the far end of the basement."

He had stayed there for the best part of an hour while Abbott had gone back and forth to collect a large number of wooden boxes from their temporary storage place under the stairwell. When finally satisfied that the coast was clear, Turnock had emerged from his hiding place and returned to the fourth floor to find that apparently no one had used the lift in the meantime. Two minutes later he had walked out of the building, vastly relieved that the duty constable hadn't thought to ask what had kept him so long.

"You were lucky, Bill."

"In more ways than one," said Turnock. "I had a grandstand view when Abbott returned a file he'd borrowed from the historical section. I checked it after he'd left, and guess what? It was a profile of Eisenhower from '42 to '45."

"What am I supposed to deduce from that?" Deakin asked calmly.

"I would have thought the answer was pretty obvious. Winter has been looking for ways and means to persuade Eisenhower to see reason and now he's found an angle he can exploit."

"Between the covers of an old file? You'll have to do better than that, Bill."

"The file was stuffed thick with memorabilia, memos, semi-official letters, and Orders of the Day, all drafted in Eisenhower's own hand. Believe me, there were more than enough examples to guide the penman."

"The penman?" Deakin said mockingly. "I hadn't realized he was involved too."

"Use your brains, George. Why else would Abbott turn the storeroom into a drawing office? Look, the way I see it, Winter told the penman to forge some incriminating evidence which he could use against Eisenhower."

"What sort of evidence?"

Turnock rumpled his hair. "How the hell should I know? I'm not a mind reader."

"A scandal," Deakin mused. "One big enough to guarantee that Eisenhower would not be returned to the White House for a second term if the voters got wind of it."

"Some hangover from the war." Turnock seized on Deakin's theme and began to develop it. "Some major controversy which would put him in a very bad light. Something he did that was out of character." He snapped his fingers. "That deserter—the only soldier to be executed for cowardice in the face of the enemy. What was his name? Slovik—Eddie Slovik?"

Deakin thought the Slovik affair was unlikely to have a major impact and if memory served him right, the case had anyway been aired quite recently in the press. No, it had to be a scandal from the past, perhaps an involvement with another woman. He recalled that there had been a certain amount of gossip going the rounds of GHQ Middle East Land Forces at the time of the Cairo conference in November '43. General Marshall had dispatched a C54 to fetch Eisenhower from Algiers and he had arrived with some of his personal staff, including a bevy of WAC officers and an English girl from the Motor Transport Corps. Marshall had insisted that Eisenhower take a few days of well-earned rest after the conference was over and he had gone on a sight-seeing tour to Luxor and Karnak. There had also been an expedition to Jerusalem, Bethlehem, and the Garden of Gethsemane, but the details were hazy in his mind and he couldn't remember exactly who had been in Eisenhower's party on either occasion.

"How about it, George? Will you come with me if I take it up with Control?"

"What?" Deakin looked up, alarmed.

"Winter has got to be stopped," Turnock explained impatiently. "I want to know if I can count on your support."

"I see. What precisely are you going to say to Control? That you signed the audit proceedings of the Imprest Account even though you received some very unsatisfactory answers to your questions? That you have reason to believe Abbott turned one of the storerooms into a temporary drawing office?"

"Winter is running an illegal operation." The color began to rise in Turnock's face, steadily toning in with his gingery-red hair and mustache. "You know it as well as I do."

"I know nothing of the kind. I've heard a lot of wild accusations but I haven't been shown one shred of evidence."

"Oh, for Christ's sake, George, what more proof do you need?"

"If you were still a policeman, you'd have to make out a

much better case than the one you've got now." Deakin leaned forward, elbows on the desk, shoulders hunched, a judicious expression on his weather-beaten face. "Look," he said in a conspiratorial voice, "let's assume for the moment that Winter does intend to blackmail Eisenhower. The first question we have to ask ourselves is: How will he set about it? Obviously he would have to pass the word to Eisenhower that if he didn't get off our backs in this Suez business, he'd give the story to the newspapers. I think you'd agree Winter couldn't very well do that from this side of the Atlantic."

"He'll probably send Abbott or Hedley over to New York," said Turnock.

"Well, if you're right, Bill, and this is an illegal operation, Winter can hardly go himself. Nor can he involve the New York office, which means he's got to make all the necessary arrangements himself—airline tickets, traveler's checks, hotel reservations, and so on." Deakin clucked his tongue. "What's the name of that travel agency we've used in the past for semi-official business?"

"Trans Globe." Turnock fingered his droopy mustache, his beady eyes narrowing to pinpoints. Then the penny dropped and he gave a low whistle. "My God, that's it," he breathed. "We can get all the proof we need from the travel agency."

"You'll need to be discreet," Deakin warned. "If I were you, I'd steer clear of Miles Abbott."

"You're a regular Dutch uncle, George." Turnock got to his feet and returned the chair to its rightful place. "One thing I discovered a long time ago is that there is more than one way to skin a cat."

"But you have to catch it first."

Turnock snorted. "Do you want the door left open?" he asked.

"Yes, please." Deakin lowered his head and picked up his pen again, a none too subtle hint to Turnock that he had more pressing matters to attend to.

Alone and undisturbed, he rounded off the brief and put the

folders aside. For several minutes, Deakin sat there uncertain what to do about his former protégé; then reasoning that he had to see Winter anyway, he decided that a few timely words of warning would not come amiss. Reaching for the telephone, he called Winter's PA and asked when it would be convenient to see him.

From the moment his PA informed him that Control had a foul cold and wouldn't be coming into the office, Winter had known it was going to be one of those bloody awful Mondays when every scrap of news was certain to be either thoroughly depressing or downright bad.

The airmail package from New York had been a case in point, for although the local office had provided him with the information he'd asked for, there had been a very big fly in the ointment. Attached to the list of unsolved burglaries which had occurred in Manhattan during the previous two months was a letter which began "My Dear Charles" and went on to say that the N.Y.P.D. was puzzled to know why the enclosed statistics should be of interest to the Home Office in London and would he please furnish a satisfactory explanation. The word "satisfactory" had been underlined twice, leaving him in no doubt that both the New York office and the N.Y.P.D. wanted to know why the request had not been submitted by Scotland Yard through the usual channels. New York had asked the unanswerable and there was only one way to deal with such an inquiry. On his way out of the office to attend a meeting of the Joint Intelligence Committee at the Foreign Office, he had calmly dropped the cover letter into the secret waste destructor.

The Joint Intelligence Committee meeting chaired by Bracecourt had been notable for two things; it had lasted slightly under an hour and he had remained silent throughout. He had just sat there with a sinking feeling in the pit of his stomach as the three Service members catalogued their respective states of readiness. The fleet carriers *Eagle*, *Albion*, and *Bulwark* en route to Malta to link up with the helicopter carriers *Ocean* and *Theseus* added up to more than mere flag-waving. The salvage fleet now assembling at Gibraltar, the strike force of *Valiant* jet bombers deployed in Malta, and the *Hastings* and *Valetta* transports marshaled on Nicosia Airport in support of the Sixteenth Parachute Brigade could hardly be described as a bluff to his way of thinking. Despite Bracecourt's whispered aside, that he still thought Eden would step back from the brink, Winter had come away from the meeting convinced that it was only a question of days before the shooting started.

Returning to his office, he had succeeded in annoying his PA by rearranging the appointments she had made in his absence. First come, first served was not always a desirable way of doing business, and with a characteristic stroke of his pen, he had promoted Deakin to the top of the list. Although it was highly doubtful if the news from Hungary would make a great deal of difference, he had thought it advisable to hear George out before he set the operation in motion. It was a lousy morning for making important decisions, but unless there was a small miracle, Abbott would have to leave for New York early on Wednesday morning, a good thirty-six hours ahead of Hedley. While a reminder was scarcely necessary, he had nevertheless ringed the dates in pencil and was still gazing at the two neat circles when Deakin knocked on the door and, responding to a grunt, walked into his office.

"I'm sorry, Charles." Deakin hovered uncertainly. "I can come back later if you're busy."

"I'm never too busy to see you, George." Winter hastily closed his diary and waved him to a chair. "I hear things are heating up in Budapest?"

"They certainly are, judging by the number of cables we've had from Toby Johnston over the weekend." Deakin half rose from his chair to offer Winter the notes he'd made. "Perhaps you'd like to read this short brief, Charles?" he said.

"I'd rather you told me about it."

Deakin nodded and sat down again. Anxious to keep it short, he briefed Winter about the manifesto and the student meeting at the Polytechnic before coming to the massive demonstration which was scheduled to take place the following day.

"Do you think the government will ban it?" Winter asked when he'd finished.

"It's possible. We know they've placed three provincial regiments on full alert." Deakin rubbed his jaw. "After what has happened in Poland, I have a hunch that Gerö and his colleagues may feel they've got to reassure Khrushchev that he has a staunch ally in the Hungarian Communist Party."

"Supposing the demonstrators ignore the ban, George? Can Gerö rely on the army?"

"To maintain law and order? Well, assuming what we've heard is right about the state of morale in the armed forces, I doubt if they will open fire on their own people. If faced with open rebellion, I imagine the Central Committee will ask the Soviet Army to intervene."

"And will they?"

"It rather depends on how the Kremlin believes the Americans would react in such a situation."

Unlike Poland, Hungary bordered a neutral country, a geographical fact that was bound to worry Khrushchev. Knowing the Soviet leader's mentality, Winter guessed Khrushchev would need a lot of convincing before he accepted the view that the United States would respect Austrian neutrality.

Deakin said, "Somehow I can't see the Americans marching on Budapest, at least not without the approval of the United Nations."

"I agree with you, George." Winter fell silent. Korea had been a fluke and the General Assembly would never sanction the use of force again in a million years. A mild slap on the wrist was about the most they would consider administering to the Soviet Union, but it would be a vastly different story if Britain and France attacked Egypt.

Deakin cleared his throat. "There is another matter I would like to discuss with you," he said hesitantly.

"Oh yes, what's that?"

"Well, it concerns Bill Turnock." Deakin swallowed nervously. "I'm afraid he's been shooting his mouth off."

"What about?"

"Our Middle East policy. You see, Bill is opposed to the use of force and, like the rest of us, he knows we're a party to this secret alliance between France and Israel." Deakin felt the sweat oozing from both palms and wiped them against his knees. "I'm worried that he may do something stupid."

"And you'd like me to have a word with him?"

"If you would," Deakin said miserably.

"Leave it to me." Winter said coldly. "I'll be very diplomatic."

11.

Deakin inspected his appearance in the full-length mirror. The dark gray, single-breasted suit was a little old-fashioned, but then so was he. Narrow lapels and tapered slacks might be all the rage these days but with his spindly legs he would look ridiculous in drainpipe trousers. Nor could he see himself wearing a narrow knitted tie and suede shoes. Only teddy boys with velvet collars to their jackets, and men like Winter who looked absurdly young for their age, could get away with that sort of thing. Give him a silk tie with discreet stripes and a pair of black leather, lace-up shoes any day.

"You look very smart, George."

"Yes. Well, I must admit this suit does look as good as new, Marjorie." Deakin stepped back from the mirror and closed the wardrobe. "Thank you, dear."

"For what?" she asked.

"For pressing it so neatly."

"I didn't." Marjorie picked up a tiny brush and rubbed it in the mascara. "It's just come back from the dry cleaner's. I took it in on Saturday."

"They were very quick." Deakin glanced at his wristwatch and wondered how much longer Marjorie would be. Alan and

June Squires had invited them for seven and it was past 6:30 already.

"I'll be ready in another five minutes, George," she said, answering his unspoken question.

Deakin nodded. "Shall I wait for you downstairs?"

"Zip me up first."

"A pleasure," he said gallantly and came up behind her. The thin shoulder straps of Marjorie's ivory-colored satin slip had an unnerving effect on him and he fumbled with the zipper. Slowly, his hand shaking, he drew it up to the neck.

"You needn't bother with the hook and eye, George. I can manage it."

"Just as well," he mumbled. "I'm all fingers and thumbs." Deakin placed both hands on Marjorie's shoulders and gazed at her reflection in the dressing table mirror.

"You're a very kind and thoughtful man, George."

"Am I?" he said huskily.

"And generous too." Marjorie reached up and stroked his wrists. "Coral is a very lucky girl. She doesn't deserve such an expensive present."

"Oh, you mean the camera I've got her for Christmas?"

"Yes. It must have cost you a small fortune."

"Actually I got it at a bargain price. The shop was having a closing-down sale." Her hands were cool and soft, her touch light and sensuous as it had been that last evening of the winter holiday in Zermatt when, in the privacy of his room, they had explored each other's bodies for the first time. "I know Christmas is still two months away," he said hoarsely, "but it was too good an opportunity to miss." Her hand deftly undoing his fly and slipping inside as he cupped her breasts in wonder. He closed his eyes, remembering that moment in time as if it were only yesterday.

"Now you just stop that, George."

"Stop what?"

"What you're doing." Marjorie's face smiled at him in the mirror. "Let's save it for tonight," she murmured, and gently removed his hands.

"I—I'm sorry," he stammered. "It's that perfume you're wearing. It reminded me of Zermatt."

She smiled knowingly. "Later, George," she said.

"Yes, later." Deakin turned away and walked out of the bedroom, flushed and embarrassed at his behavior. He knew himself to be something of a cold-blooded fish and he couldn't understand what had made him fondle Marjorie in such a suggestive manner. Pawing her body the way he had put him on the same level with those disgusting middle-aged men in drab raincoats who prowled the back streets of Soho ogling the prostitutes standing in shop doorways. Taking a deep breath, he went downstairs into the living room.

Coral was sitting in front of the fire, her eyes glued to the television, a pile of exercise books awaiting correction on a table beside her. Feeling like an interloper, Deakin sat down on the couch, as far removed from his stepdaughter as the tiny room would allow. Her eyes briefly registered his presence and then returned to the fourteen-inch screen.

"How was school today?" Deakin asked politely.

"Do you mind? I'm listening to Eisenhower."

Suitably rebuked, Deakin retreated into his shell and with half an ear, listened to an election speech that Eisenhower had given the day before at the Sheraton-Park Hotel in Washington. There were times when he wondered how such a malleable and loving woman as Marjorie could have produced such an ill-mannered and spiteful little bitch as Coral. Like father, like son must, he thought, apply equally to daughters. Certainly it was the only logical explanation he could think of. It was a good thing he and Marjorie were going out to dinner because if he had to suffer one more abrasive remark, Coral might wish she'd never been born. With Turnock riding his favorite hobby horse and acting the great detective, he'd had just about all he could take for one day: Bill and his bloody proof that Winter was running an illegal operation, Bill calling for a showdown and demanding that he should support him. It was a good thing Control was off sick, otherwise Bill would have dragged him down into the mire. He didn't wish the great man any harm, but the longer Control stayed away from the office, the happier he would be. After his timely warning, he had hoped that Winter would have a few words with Turnock and bring him to his senses but for some reason, Charles seemed to be dragging his feet.

"I'm ready when you are, George."

Rescued in the nick of time, Deakin thought, and rose to his feet with alacrity. "What a smart coat, Marjorie," he said warmly. "It really suits you."

"You've seen me in it before, George. Lots of times."

"Have I, dear?" Deakin shook his head in disbelief. "I thought it was new."

"That only proves how unobservant you are," Coral snapped waspishly.

Deakin bit back a retort and went out into the hall. As he struggled into his overcoat, he heard Marjorie assure Coral that they would be home before midnight in a voice which sounded as if she was asking for her daughter's permission. Asserting his authority for once, he returned to the living room and taking Marjorie by the elbow, steered her toward the front door.

"Good-bye, Coral," he called out in a loud voice. "Don't wait up for us."

"Don't worry, I won't."

"Good," he snapped and slammed the door behind him. He knew it was a somewhat childish display of temper but he felt better for it.

"Good for you, George." Marjorie slipped her arm through his and hugged it tight. "It's about time you put your foot down with Coral."

"Hmmm," he said.

"What does 'hmmm' mean?" Marjorie asked.

"It means we are going to be very late unless we get a move on."

"It's only just after 6:45, George."

"I know that, dear, but the Squires live in Highgate and that is at least half an hour on the tube."

Turning the corner at the top of Queen's Road, Deakin began to increase the length of his stride. By the time they neared the Underground station at Hendon Central, Marjorie was almost running to keep up with him. So too was the Special Branch officer who was following them at an interval of fifty yards to their rear.

Hedley stared at the television screen, the glass of whiskey in his hand still untouched. The film had been shot by an amateur with a handheld 8mm camera with the result that the sequences were jerky and the pictures frequently out of focus, but it was the first and only newsreel so far of the uprising in Budapest.

It opened with a panoramic view of the massive number of demonstrators who had gathered outside the Gothic-style Parliament House in Kossuth Square at five o'clock on Tuesday evening, and then cut to the radio station on Brody Sandor Street where the AVH had fired on a crowd of students. Taken some hours later and filmed in almost total darkness with only a glimmer of background light from the gas lamps in the narrow cobbled street, the overall effect was like some obscure impressionist painting. It was just possible to make out the shattered oak gates of the main entrance to the radio station which had been rammed with a car, and beyond them the rococo four-story house which served as the administrative offices.

The lighting was better in the third and final scene, which suggested it had been shot by a different photographer some hours before the students had stormed the radio station demanding that their manifesto be broadcast over the air. Taken in the vicinity of the municipal park, it showed a splinter group of demonstrators attacking the fifty-foot bronze statue of Stalin. A workman was using a blowtorch on one of the legs while others attached steel cables round the neck. Two winch trucks took up the slack, the hawsers stretched to the breaking point, and then suddenly the head snapped off. The cables were repositioned around the body, the trucks moved forward again, and the massive trunk toppled to the ground, leaving only the boots still planted in the pink marble base.

The film ended and was replaced by a sketch map of Hungary showing the position of Budapest in relation to Szekesfehervar, a town forty miles southwest of the capital, and Cegled, which was approximately the same distance to the east. A disembodied voice informed Hedley that JS III and T43 tanks had entered Budapest from both directions in the early hours of Wednesday morning. A squadron of tanks which had halted for a short time at the Moricz Zsigmond Circus on the Buda side of the river had eventually crossed the Danube into Pest by the Margaret Bridge and were now patrolling the embankment between Parliament House and the Duma Hotel.

"The situation is extremely confused," the reporter continued, "but it is known that Ernö Gerö has stepped down in favor of Imre Nagy who assumed the office of Prime Minister in the early hours of this morning. It is also a fact that the Hungarian Army and Civil Police are unwilling to take any action against the rioters. Indeed, there have been a number of instances where troops and police have actually joined forces with the insurgents against the AVH. The question most Hungarians are now asking themselves is: Who requested the Soviet Army to intervene and will they withdraw from the city?"

Hedley leaned forward and switched off the television set. *There was*, he thought, *no prize for guessing the answer to that question.* Gerö might have installed Nagy as Prime Minister but he was still the First Secretary of the Communist Party, the only office with any real power. Nagy was both a sop to the revolutionaries and a lifesaver for the Central Committee who were determined to preserve the existing structure. Always a man to hedge his bets, Gerö had undoubtedly asked the Kremlin to back his shaky administration with Soviet troops.

There were two Red Army divisions stationed in Hungary, the Second and Seventeenth Motorized, and neither formation was suited to the task it had been given. The 45-ton JS III tanks would be fairly effective in the wide boulevards but only while they were in transit from one end of the avenue to the other, and they would be singularly vulnerable in the dusty back streets. Without infantry to support them, there was nothing to prevent the insurgents from reoccupying the ground they had just cleared; without infantry to back them up, the tanks could be picked off one by one as they rumbled through the narrow alleyways. If Khrushchev intended to crush the uprising, he would have to throw in a lot more than two divisions top-heavy with armor.

The telephone rang suddenly, breaking the brooding silence in the room and causing Hedley to flinch involuntarily, so that some of the whiskey slopped over the glass and ran down his fingers. It pealed four times and then stopped. Exactly sixty seconds later it trilled one more time. Leaving the glass on the mantelpiece, he collected his raincoat from the hall and let himself out of the flat.

Winter had taken over from Abbott as his control officer, but the drill hadn't changed. Strolling up to Kensington High Street, he entered the Underground station and, having shut himself in one of the phone booths near the ticket office, dialed the Four Square Laundry.

Marjorie frowned at her empty glass and wondered if she dare have another gin and tonic.

"Come on, be a devil for once." Alan Squires pried her fingers loose and removed the glass. "Another little drink won't do you any harm."

"I must have had at least three already."

"So who's counting?"

"I am." Marjorie smiled. "And I think you're trying to get me drunk."

"Shush." Squires put a finger to his lips. "Don't let June hear you say that or she'll think I have designs on you."

"And have you?" she asked as he started to move away.

"Time will tell," he said vaguely, "time will tell."

Marjorie sat down on one arm of the settee. Her legs felt as though they were made of cotton wool and her speech was definitely becoming slurred. It was ridiculous that three gin and tonics should affect her this way, but of course she had been drinking on an empty stomach. She would have had a glass of milk before they left if only George had thought to warn her that the Squires were asking some of their neighbors in for a drink before dinner. The invitation had said seven for 7:30 and unless her eyes deceived her, it was now ten minutes to nine according to the Westminster clock on the mantelpiece above the Adam fireplace. When were they going to eat, for goodness' sake? Or had she got it wrong? Was it dinner or a cocktail party the Squires were giving? Leaning sideways, she helped herself to a handful of salted peanuts from a silver bowl on the coffee table.

"Your drink, sweetie."

Marjorie looked up. No one had called her that in years and while Alan was perhaps a trifle too attentive, it was very flattering to the ego. He was taller than George and so much better looking, although she had to admit there was just a suspicion of a double chin. "Why, thank you, Alan," she said demurely.

"My pleasure." Squires looked round the room, his brown eyes narrowing behind the horn-rimmed glasses. "Some people never know when to leave, do they?" he murmured.

"Who do you mean?"

"The Duckworths—the couple over there talking to George. Soon as they go, we can push off to the Mirabel."

Marjorie lowered her glass, frowning. "Where?" she asked in a thick voice.

"The Mirabel. I thought I'd make things easy for June, so we're eating out. Michael and Elizabeth Wilde are coming with us."

Marjorie couldn't remember whether she had been introduced to the Wildes. The drawing room had been full of people when they'd arrived and she had been quite overwhelmed by the sea of strange faces, but now that all the guests had departed with the exception of the Duckworths, she had no difficulty in identifying the Wildes. Elizabeth Wilde was wearing a deceptively simple black dress, probably from Norman Hartnell or Hardy Amies, she thought. No matter which, it had obviously cost her husband a small fortune, but then the people who lived in Highgate Village weren't short of a bob or two. Neither was Alan, for all that he was a civil servant like George. She supposed he must have made a lot of money for himself when he was working for the Arabs.

"Don't look now." Squires raised his head and froze, pointing like a gun dog. "But I do believe the Duckworths are leaving."

A light showed in the doorway of the mock Georgian residence across the road and, reacting swiftly, the Special Branch man retreated farther into the shadow, pressing himself against the stone wall behind him as if hoping to become part of it. He had been watching the house in Highgate Avenue for close on an hour and a half and was frozen to the marrow, but now it looked as though the last of the determined drinkers were leaving the party. Completely fed up and bored, he watched two couples move off in opposite directions and wondered how much longer it would be before the Deakins appeared.

Five minutes passed and then another five. A light showed in the doorway again and in the still night air he could hear the faint sound of laughter and the murmur of voices. The light went out, doors opened and closed, and a car engine fired into life. Headlights appeared to his right and presently a Daimler saloon drove past the house, the driver sounding the horn three times in rapid succession. As the Daimler began to pick up speed, a Vauxhall Cresta emerged from the driveway of the mock Georgian residence and followed it down the hill.

In twelve years on the force the Special Branch man had acquired a wide vocabulary of expletives, but as he watched the taillights disappear into the distance there just weren't enough four-letter words to express his feelings adequately.

* * *

Hedley left the Underground station, crossed over the road and turned right, heading toward the Holborn Viaduct. Although reasonably satisfied that nobody was following him, he decided it would do no harm to run one more check, and, wheeling into Procter Street, he walked as far as the next intersection before doubling back on his tracks. Still playing it safe, he circled Red Lion Square in a clockwise direction and approached Winter's Jaguar from the rear. Drawing alongside the car, he opened the door and ducking his head under the sill, got inside.

"Better late than never," Winter said and pressed the starter.

"It wasn't easy to shake our friends off my tail."

"I don't suppose it was. Tom McNulty doesn't suffer fools gladly." Winter glanced into the rearview mirror and then pulled out from the curb. Making a series of left-hand turns, he proceeded along High Holborn toward the Viaduct. "Are you sure you lost them?" he asked presently.

"I switched trains at Paddington, Baker Street, and Oxford Circus before I caught one to Holborn on the Central Line. If that didn't throw them off, I don't see what else I could have done." Hedley fetched out a packet of Benson and Hedges from his raincoat pocket and lit a cigarette with the lighter in the dashboard. "Anyway, why have we suddenly changed our policy? I mean, until this evening you wanted me to lead them round by the nose."

"I still do, but I don't want McNulty to know that I'm deputizing for Abbott."

Hedley said, "That's something I've been meaning to ask you. What's happened to Miles?"

"He's no longer with us, James; he left for New York this morning." Winter opened the glove compartment and passed a large brown envelope to him. "And you're going to be joining him."

"When?"

"You're booked on the 2230 BOAC flight tomorrow night."

Hedley opened the envelope and found that it contained an airline ticket issued by the Trans Globe Travel Agency, a reservation slip for the Algonquin Hotel on West Forty-fourth

Street, and a wad of dollar bills.

"Count them," said Winter. "You should have $850."

"How long am I supposed to make it last?"

"A week, perhaps ten days. It depends how soon Abbott can run Walter Emsden to ground." Winter signaled that he was turning right, changed down into third, and swung into St. Andrew's Street. "Emsden is a man of many parts," he said, preempting the inevitable question. "Author, reviewer, and features editor of *Rod and Gun* magazine. He's also a stringer for a syndicated gossip columnist and a pretty shady character. Two reasons why we need him."

"And we've got a story for this Emsden. Right?"

"That's certainly the impression we want to give Eisenhower's campaign manager. You've led the CIA to Telegraph Cottage, Wyecroft Farm, Reims, and La Bouée Hotel; now you're going to lead them to Walter Emsden. You will tell Emsden that you possess a number of letters which seem to indicate that the president was having an affair with Kay Summersby. This won't come as any surprise to him because a similar tale was going the rounds in Washington before D day. What will surprise him is your revelation that this wartime romance was still going strong in September '51."

"I see."

Winter frowned. Hedley was something of an enigma and his noncommittal voice offered no clue as to what he was actually thinking. He was shrewd enough to guess what was in the wind, yet so far he had done everything that had been asked of him, never once voicing an objection. However, despite his apparent complicity, Winter sensed he would need to tread warily.

"If your meeting with Emsden provokes the kind of reaction I think it will, then it can only be a matter of hours before McNulty's people come knocking on your door."

"You want to know something?" Hedley opened the vent and tossed his cigarette out into the road. "I won't answer the door unless you come clean about this job."

"We're running a black operation." Winter twisted his

mouth in a sour grimace. "At least, that's how we describe it in the trade. Others would say that blackmail is a more apt description. The difference is, we're not asking for money. All we want is silence."

"From Eisenhower," said Hedley.

"Well, he's the only man who can hold Dulles in check when the storm breaks, and break it will because sometime during the next fortnight the Israelis will launch a preemptive war against Egypt. The government is confident they will destroy the Egyptian Army in the Sinai and as soon as their spearheads are within striking distance of the Canal we and the French will land at Suez to separate the belligerents."

"We must be mad. No one in his right mind is going to swallow that story."

Winter relaxed his grip on the steering wheel. In two short sentences Hedley had made it very clear that they were two of a kind. The subterfuge aroused no feeling of moral indignation in either of them, only a sense of incredulity that the government was naïve enough to believe they could get away with it.

"If we invade Egypt the United Nations will have a field day."

"We can weather that, Hedley."

"But not a sustained run on the pound."

"Sterling will only come under pressure if Eisenhower gives the word."

"But if this operation is successful, he won't?"

"That is one of our objectives," said Winter. "We also need the protection of their nuclear umbrella because, as sure as God made little apples, Khrushchev won't be able to resist getting in on the act."

"These letters Eisenhower is supposed to have written," Hedley said thoughtfully. "Surely our friends in Grosvenor Square must know they're fakes?"

"So what if they do? For every expert who says the letters are forgeries, there will be one who's prepared to swear they're genuine. McNulty knows this and that's why he can't afford to take any chances."

Hedley turned away and stared out of the window. "I wonder where the hell we're going," he said quietly.

"I'm making a circular tour. We crossed the river at Blackfriars Bridge and turned west. Right now we're running parallel with the Albert Embankment."

"I was referring to the operation. I think it stinks."

"So do I," said Winter, "but we don't have any choice. The State Department isn't interested in Hungary because Dulles has climbed onto the anticolonial bandwagon."

Winter's face clouded in anger and the venom welled and began to spill over. Dulles, the statesman who wanted America's supremacy to be moral as well as thermonuclear. Dulles, the self-righteous corporation lawyer who had insisted on masterminding every move and whose achievements included the failure of the Baghdad Pact, Soviet penetration of Egypt, and the nationalization of the Canal. Dulles was a dissembler, a man so devious, so incapable of doing anything straight that no one knew what he intended to do next.

"You and I may not like what we're doing," Winter said in conclusion, "but after the hand we've been dealt, I don't think we need feel guilty about it."

"It's not going to be a repeat of the Crabb affair, is it?" Hedley asked quietly.

"I didn't mastermind that foul-up," Winter said. "I've never bungled an operation yet."

They were talking at cross-purposes again. He'd wanted to know if the operation had been sanctioned by the Foreign Office, but either Winter had failed to see the inference or else he had deliberately misinterpreted it. He wondered if he should ask him point-blank if they had official clearance but on reflection, decided it would be a waste of time. No matter how Winter answered his question, he'd never know whether it was the truth or a barefaced lie. In any case, if the operation was successful no one would give a damn whether or not it had been authorized; if it was a failure, the SIS would disown him anyway.

"All right," said Hedley. "Suppose you tell me exactly what I have to do in New York."

12.

Deakin massaged his temples, seeking relief from
a blinding headache which, contrary to Marjorie's opinion,
stemmed from nervous tension rather than a hangover from the
night before. Aspirins and strong black coffee had failed to
alleviate the pain before he left the house, and while Deakin
hadn't expected to find peace and quiet at the office, he had
hoped that at least Bill Turnock would leave him alone.

"I assume you know that Control is still on the sick list?"
he said morosely.

"I do." Turnock closed the door behind him and drew up a
chair. "I'm here because I need your advice, George."

"What about?"

"I think I'm being followed."

Deakin stared at Turnock, his headache temporarily forgotten. "You think?" he repeated. "That means you're not sure."

"I may not be a hundred percent certain, George, but it's not
a figment of my imagination, if that's what you're thinking."

"I'm not," said Deakin. "I've never been one to jump to conclusions, Bill. I like to hear the facts before I make up my
mind."

"That's the trouble, George. I don't really have any facts."
Turnock sniffed, then said, "Do you remember me asking you

about Sven Uddenberg?"

"Of course I do. He's the London representative for Middle East Airlines. As I recall, he invited you to dinner in your capacity as Head of the Arabian Desk. It's a once-a-year thing."

"So you told me. Anyway, the invitation was for last night, and because the Uddenbergs were expecting us at seven I told Joan I would change at the office and meet her at Waterloo Station."

The arrangement had saved him an unnecessary journey, and without the car he'd figured they could leave the party at a reasonable hour, making the excuse that they had to catch the last train to West Byfleet.

"I told Joan she'd find me outside W. H. Smith & Son opposite platform 7, and it was while I was waiting for her to arrive that I began to have this itchy feeling that somebody was watching me."

The itchy feeling had persisted, and as he discreetly observed the people around him, his suspicions had been aroused by a slim, youngish-looking man in a dark blue duffle coat who hastily looked the other way whenever he glanced in his direction.

"The Uddenbergs live in Sussex Gardens," Turnock continued, "and after Joan arrived at 6:40, he followed us down to the Underground. He was still with us when we changed on to the Central Line at Tottenham Court Road, but I lost track of him after we got out at Lancaster Gate."

There had been no sign of the man in the dark blue duffle coat when they'd left the Uddenbergs' flat in Sussex Gardens and as far as Turnock was aware nobody had followed them home to West Byfleet. It was only when he took their Yorkshire terrier for a brief run around the garden before going to bed that he realized he'd been mistaken.

"He was standing under one of the elm trees on the common, George. At first he was no more than a blurred outline, but then he moved and I saw his cigarette glowing in the darkness."

"You don't know that it was the same man," said Deakin. "It could have been someone else—perhaps a peeping Tom."

"I'd like to believe there was no connection but every instinct contradicts it."

"What else do your instincts tell you?"

"Not a lot." Turnock shrugged his shoulders. "Obviously Winter must be on to me. Some bloody clerk at the Trans Globe Travel Agency must have told him I'd been sniffing around."

"Poking your nose into official business that didn't concern you," Deakin said in an icy voice.

"Official? What the hell are you talking about, George? You know damned well that what Winter's running is illegal."

"I know that you've had a bee in your bonnet ever since you returned from Paris with the news that the French were arming the Israelis for a surprise attack on Egypt. Abbott fails to satisfy your queries about certain entries he made in the Imprest Account, and suddenly there's a conspiracy, one which gradually draws in more and more people until we reach the point where Special Branch is involved."

"Special Branch?" Turnock echoed in a hollow voice.

"Well, who else could have been following you? Some probationer from the Training Wing?"

"It's possible. Winter could have told the commandant that it was a training exercise."

"Now you're clutching at straws." Deakin wagged an admonishing finger at Turnock. "Face the truth, Bill, you're wrong about Winter. He may be running a black operation but I'm sure it's legal. That's why he was able to call in Special Branch when you showed your hand."

Turnock was slow to grasp the implications at first, but when the penny finally dropped, the color drained from his face. "I've landed myself in the shit, haven't I, George?" he said hoarsely.

"Right up to your neck," Deakin agreed.

"Oh, my God, what am I going to do?"

"You could change your attitude."

"What?"

"You're too pro-Arab," said Deakin, "too quick to see their

point of view. Everybody in this building knows what you think of Eden's policy, but I suggest you try cultivating a little enthusiasm for it. Do an about-face, pretend you've seen the light and are now in favor of the Suez invasion. Dig up every scrap of evidence you can to prove that Nasser takes his orders from the Kremlin and show it to Winter."

"Are you suggesting that I lick his boots, George?"

"No, but I think you should try to curry a little favor. Of course you'll have to be a bit more subtle about it than you've been so far. Winter is no fool and he'd soon smell a rat if you were too obsequious."

"I don't know, George," Turnock said, frowning. "Somehow I can't see myself crawling to him. Maybe I should have a word with Control and put him straight when he returns to the office?"

"Don't be an idiot," Deakin snapped. "What are you going to say to him? 'please, sir, I've been spying on your deputy because I thought he was up to no good'? Do that and you'll surely be digging a grave for yourself."

"Perhaps."

"There's no perhaps about it." Deakin rubbed his eyes. The top of his head felt as though it were about to lift off and the pain was beginning to affect his vision. "I've given you my advice," he said wearily. "The rest is up to you."

"I've never crawled to anybody in my life, but I suppose there's a first time for everything."

The telephone had started ringing soon after Winter arrived at the office and from then on there had been no letup. Brace-court, the Cabinet Office, the Director of Naval Intelligence, and Edmunds, the Commandant of the Training Wing at Gerrards Cross; as soon as one caller hung up, the switchboard operator put through another. Answering the phone yet again, he found he had Cleaver on the line.

"About this private arrangement of ours," said Cleaver. "At long last there've been a couple of developments—one promising, the other negative. Which do you want to hear first?"

Winter said, "Let's start on an optimistic note. It hasn't been a very good morning so far."

"You've no cause for optimism, Charles, at least not where Turnock is concerned. He and his wife had dinner with the Uddenbergs last night. Sven Uddenberg works for Middle East Airlines."

"So what's the bottom line, Malcolm?" said Winter. "Something tells me there has to be one."

"The bottom line is that Uddenberg and Mr. Abdul Aziz Rida are bosom pals. They've known one another for years."

"Was Rida at this dinner party?" Winter asked sharply.

"No, he was elsewhere, painting the town red. Mind you, if you think about it, Rida didn't have to be there, did he?"

Winter grimaced. What was it Cleaver had said to him when they'd set up the surveillance operation almost a fortnight ago? "Of course you do realize we'll only be skimming the surface? I mean, your worm in the apple could contact Rida through an intermediary."

"You're right," he said tersely. "Uddenberg is probably the go-between."

"Yes, well, that brings me to the Deakins. They went to a cocktail party in Highgate given by a Mr. and Mrs. Alan Squires. The party broke up around nine o'clock and then the Squires took them out to dinner."

"Where?"

"I knew you'd ask that embarrassing question." There was a momentary pause while Cleaver hemmed and hawed, seemingly reluctant to admit that there had been a foul-up. Finally he said, "I'm afraid we lost them. Our man was on foot and the Deakins and the Squires drove off in a car. Maybe it should have occurred to him that the Deakins might be going on somewhere later, but nobody is infallible and we all make mistakes."

"I hope that's not a portent of things to come," said Winter.

"This Alan Squires," Cleaver said briskly, determined to end the postmortem. "We don't have anything on him. Do you want me to look into his background?"

"How are you placed?"

"For manpower?" Cleaver snorted. "The situation hasn't changed; we still don't have enough men to go round. We're not doing a very good job on Deakin and Turnock as it is."

Without actually saying so, Cleaver was inviting him to make a decision. He had to choose between Deakin and Turnock because on the evidence now available, it was both foolish and inefficient to go on hedging his bets.

"Forget Deakin," said Winter. "Concentrate on Turnock and let's give him the full treatment—twenty-four-hour surveillance, mail intercept, phone tap—the lot."

"For how long?"

"Until I'm ready to string him up by his thumbs."

"But that could take weeks or even months."

"I know that, but once the fox has broken cover, you don't call off the hounds before the chase is over."

"A fox?" said Cleaver. "Is that how you see Turnock?"

"Don't you?" Winter countered.

"I suppose so. Certainly there are more question marks against Turnock than your other man but all the same, it's odd they should both choose the same evening to go out. Of course it could be just a coincidence but ever since we've been watching him, Deakin hasn't stirred out of the house except to go to the office."

"What about Turnock?"

"He took his wife to see *The Mousetrap* last Friday, but that was the only break in the usual pattern, unless you count the spot of overtime he put in on Saturday afternoon. Whatever else he may be, your Mr. Turnock is very security-conscious. It seems he couldn't remember whether he'd locked the safe in the office."

"Wait a minute," Winter said quickly. "Are you saying he'd already left the office?"

"Oh yes. He went for a beer and sandwich in the Hare and Hounds in Victoria Street."

"Thanks for telling me."

"Don't mention it," Cleaver said and hung up.

Winter slowly replaced the phone. Cleaver had been looking

for a break in the usual pattern and yet he'd seen nothing remarkable about Turnock's behavior on Saturday afternoon. Apparently it hadn't occurred to him to wonder why Turnock,
instead of going home to West Byfleet, had been drinking in
a pub around the corner from the office. Had Cleaver stopped
to think, he would have realized that Turnock's behavior had
been premeditated, that his excuse for returning to the office
was nonsense.

Winter picked up a ruler and flexed it in a bow. Abbott had
tried to warn him about Turnock but he'd preferred to believe
that Miles was making a mountain out of a molehill. He had
been too confident, too sure that all the angles had been
covered and as a result of his mindless optimism, the operation
was now in jeopardy. Just how much information Turnock had
passed on to Rida was a matter for conjecture, but clearly the
risks had been doubled, perhaps even quadrupled, and there
was nothing, absolutely nothing he could do about it. The
nature of the threat was unknown and in the circumstances,
warning Hedley and Abbott to be on their guard was a singularly useless piece of advice, one that would be more irritating
than helpful.

Nor could he take any action against Turnock; the operation
was illegal and that made him untouchable. *One day,* Winter
thought savagely, *one day I'll have him and then I'll break his
spine.* Unable to do anything positive, he vented his spleen on
the ruler, bending it double until eventually it snapped in two.

Vasili Korznikov was a full colonel in the KGB but Rida
thought few people would guess that, judging by his austere
office in the basement of 13 Kensington Palace Gardens. The
room was about twice the size of a prison cell and seemed
equally oppressive in the harsh glare from the strip light in the
ceiling, the distempered walls totally bare except for the portrait of Lenin directly behind the desk. Apart from the desk,
the only other items of furniture were a filing cabinet, a carpet, and an upright ladder-back chair which Rida found decidedly uncomfortable.

"This is a very depressing room," Korznikov said, as if reading his thoughts. "However, it is the most secure place in the entire embassy."

"I imagine it would be," Rida said dryly.

"The walls, the ceiling, and the floor are soundproof and if you look closely, you'll notice there is no ventilation system." Korznikov smiled. "In less than half an hour, the atmosphere in here will be more humid than a Turkish bath. That's why I'd like to conclude our business as quickly as possible."

"In that case, I'll come straight to the point." Rida moistened his lips. "You'll be pleased to hear that I've met our English sympathizer at last."

"When?"

"Last night, face to face in a gentleman's cloakroom where we had a short but very interesting conversation." Rida produced a small envelope from the inside pocket of his jacket and passed it to Korznikov. "He also gave me these two photographs. The man in the open-neck shirt is James Hedley, the other is Miles Abbott. According to the Englishman, they're engaged in a black operation directed against President Eisenhower."

Korznikov looked at the photographs: they were passport size and surrounded by a large black border, which suggested the Englishman had used masking tape to obscure the documents they were attached to.

"I think our friend Winter must also be involved," he said presently.

"His name wasn't mentioned during our conversation, Vasili."

"Nevertheless, we can safely assume that Winter is behind it. Black operations are his specialty; that's how he made his name." Korznikov placed the photographs to one side. "However, that's beside the point. What exactly did the Englishman tell you?"

"He said the SIS are determined that Eisenhower should cease interfering and allow the British to settle the Suez Canal dispute in their own way. To achieve this aim, pressure will be exerted on Eisenhower to ensure that he toes the line when the British and the French invade my country. The Englishman was unable to give specific details, but it seems the SIS possess a number of highly incriminating letters, supposedly written by Eisenhower, which could cost him the election if the press got hold of them."

"We certainly can't allow that to happen." Korznikov pursed his lips. "Still, it shouldn't be too difficult to recover these incriminating letters. Who's got them, Abbott or Hedley?"

"Miles Abbott," said Rida, "and he's already in New York."

The Politburo had made it very clear to Korznikov that he was to give every assistance to Rida, but his writ did not extend to New York. He would need clearance from Moscow before taking action, although the First Chief Directorate were unlikely to raise any objections. From time to time he had informed them about his meetings with Rida, but after their get-together at the Yugoslavian Embassy, their policy line had been absolutely consistent. Nasser was the key to Soviet penetration of the Middle East and it was vital he remained in power. If this meant the KGB were obliged to protect the American president, then so be it.

"Do we know where Abbott is staying?" Korznikov asked.

"He's booked into the Taft Hotel on Seventh Avenue."

Kornikov made a note of the address. A top-priority coded message to Moscow with the New York bureau as an information addressee should do the trick. A simple yes or no from Moscow would then set the wheels rapidly in motion. Bogach would probably be in charge of the operation. He was the senior KGB officer in New York, a man of vast experience who could be relied upon to do a good job. The two photographs would have to be sent over by special courier, but that shouldn't hold Bogach up. The telegram would tell him where Abbott was staying in New York and he could take it from there.

"What's Hedley's role?" he asked.

"Who knows?" Rida waved both hands, a gesture which seemed to imply that the question was irrelevant. "All the Englishman could tell me is that he's booked on the 2230

BOAC flight tonight and that he will be staying at the Algonquin Hotel in New York."

"But he is quite certain that Abbott has these letters?"

"Yes." Rida loosened his collar. The temperature had risen
while they'd been talking and the warmer atmosphere was beginning to affect him. Or was it Korznikov making him sweat?
There was something very intimidating about Vasili, the way
he looked right through you with his cruel, Asiatic eyes. "What
do you intend to do about Abbott?" he asked nervously.

"That depends on you, Aziz."

"On me?"

"There is always a price," Korznikov murmured.

"I thought that might be the case." Rida dipped into his
jacket pocket and brought out a small cassette. "Would this be
enough?" he whispered.

"Provided you also give me the name of the Englishman.
The tape recording is quite useless without it."

Rida hesitated. The Englishman could have been a very useful agent in the long term, but he was in no position to bargain. The Muhabbarat-El-Amma Intelligence organization was
incapable of mounting an operation in New York and Korznikov knew it.

"Must I, Vasili?" he asked.

"What do you think?"

Rida mulled it over, and then told Korznikov what he wanted
to know.

Winter arrived at John Lewis's Department Store on Oxford
Street shortly before five o'clock and quickly made his way up
to the restaurant on the fourth floor. The letter, addressed to
the official post office box number in Katherine's familiar hand,
had arrived with the second delivery and even before he'd
opened the envelope, there had been this sinking feeling in the
pit of his stomach. "I've made an appointment to see a specialist in Harley Street at 3:15 on Thursday afternoon," she'd
written, "and I'd be grateful if you could meet me afterward,

outside the restaurant in John Lewis's. I should be there by five." There had been no endearments and she had signed her name with the initial letter only, pressing down on the pen nib so firmly that the K had almost gone through the paper.

A specialist: Winter hadn't liked the sound of that because after a lot of argument, Katherine had agreed to see a gynecologist before she arranged to have an abortion. He had tried to phone her several times but on each occasion the Portuguese maid had told him that Mrs. Lang was out and was unable to say when she would return. Leaving a telephone number where Katherine could reach him would have been a gross breach of security and, unwilling to break the rules, he had tried to shut her out of his mind but to no avail. Now, instead of watching the clock like a man who only had a few hours to live, he elbowed a path through the crowd of shoppers on the fourth floor and followed the signs to the restaurant.

Katherine was waiting for him outside the restaurant and as he drew nearer, Winter thought how pale and drawn she looked. Her eyes were blank as if she were in a trance, an impression that gained credence when he noticed the cigarette burning down between the index and second finger of her right hand.

"Hello, Katherine," he said gently. "How are you?"

"I'm fine," she said in a voice that was completely flat. "On top of the world."

"You look it," he lied, and made to kiss her on the mouth, but at the last moment she turned her head away and his lips brushed her cheek instead. "Well now," Winter smiled and squeezed her arm affectionately, "let's find a quiet table where we can talk in private."

"The restaurant will be closing soon."

"Oh, I'm sure they'll serve us."

"I don't want anything to eat."

"Of course you don't." There was a vacant table just inside the entrance and he steered her toward it, beckoning to the nearest waitress. "A strong cup of tea, that's what you need."

"If you say so." Katherine sat down, opened her handbag, and took out a packet of Rothmans. "I'm smoking like a chimney," she said. Her attitude was defiant, as though daring him to criticize her.

"Are you?" Winter said, taking the easy way out. "Well, I must say I hadn't noticed."

"I'm not pregnant, Charles." Her voice carried to the adjoining tables and in the embarrassed silence that followed, several heads turned in their direction.

A waitress coughed discreetly to attract their attention and then asked if she could take their order. Winter said he would like a pot of tea for two and thank you, but no, they didn't want any cakes. Around them, the silence ended as suddenly as it had begun.

"I'm sorry," Katherine murmured.

"Don't be; there's nothing to be sorry about." Winter reached across the table and squeezed her hand. "What exactly did the specialist tell you?"

"He says I've got a tumor on the womb. He refused to mention the word 'cancer,' but that's what it is."

"I don't believe it."

"It's me that has to believe it, Charles, not you."

"Christ," he whispered.

"I don't think he can help me, Charles." Her mouth twisted in a bitter smile and then it all came out in halting phrases and disjointed sentences. "I went for a test on Monday at the Charing Cross Hospital. Such a nice Indian doctor, so very kind, so very gentle. He took some smears and telephoned me the following morning—after the laboratory had made their tests. He asked if I could come and see him again and we agreed I should see a specialist. I'm going into hospital tomorrow—for treatment." She jabbed her cigarette into the ashtray and crushed it to pieces. "I'm going to die, Charles."

"Nonsense," he said fiercely. "They can perform miracles these days—radium—surgery—you see, you'll be as right as rain in no time."

144

"I'm going to die," she repeated in a dull voice. "I know it."

"Oh, Christ, don't say that, Katherine."

Janet Roscoe could not recall a more boring evening than the one she had just spent. Her date, an up-and-coming press secretary, had never stopped talking about himself from the moment they'd met for dinner at the Savoy Grill until he dropped her off at her flat in Half Moon Street four long and unutterably weary hours later.

Removing her coat, she hung it up in the wardrobe and thankfully kicked off the high-heeled shoes which had been torturing her feet. About to unzip her dress, Janet had a sudden twinge of conscience and sat down on the bed, meaning to call Tom McNulty to let him know that she was back. Before she had time to lift the receiver, the telephone rang.

Answering it, she heard McNulty say, "Third time lucky, I guess."

"I'm sorry, Tom," she said contritely. "I was just about to phone you."

"Great minds think alike," said McNulty. "Did you have a good time?"

"Marvelous." *Full marks for enthusiasm,* she thought, and then added, "Thanks for standing in for me, Tom. I hope you didn't have too many calls from the duty officer."

"Only one," said McNulty. "Hedley's on his way to New York. He left on the 2230 BOAC flight."

"Oh, my God."

"No need to panic, Jan; we haven't lost him. I've arranged for the New York office to sit on his tail the moment he clears Customs and Immigration at Idlewild, and Kaplin's on the same plane."

"He's up to his old tricks again."

"Who is?"

"Hedley," she said. "Last night he managed to give us the slip, but now, twenty-four hours later, he leads Kaplin to

Heathrow. I'd really love to give that son of a bitch a piece of my mind."

"You can," said McNulty. "Tomorrow night around six o'clock eastern standard time."

"What?"

"Your plane leaves at 0900," said McNulty. "I suggest you start packing."

1956

Friday, October 26 to Monday, October 29

13.

The hairs began to rise on Abbott's neck as he handed his room key to the desk clerk. Although no one else, apart from Hedley and Winter, knew that he was staying at the Taft Hotel in New York, he had a premonition that somewhere in the lobby, somebody was watching him. Slowly he turned about and began to search the foyer from right to left. His gaze shifted from the man sprawled in an armchair reading the *New York Times*, to the two women deep in conversation at a coffee table, to the bellboy, to the people waiting by the elevators and the group of businessmen by the newsstand. All he could see was a number of innocent-looking people, but the itchy feeling persisted and grew even stronger when he went out into the street.

Abbott told himself that it was pure imagination but after a moment's reflection he decided it was better to be safe than sorry. Walking south on Seventh Avenue for two blocks, he turned left and headed east on Forty-eighth Street. Reaching the Avenue of the Americas, he turned north and began to retrace his steps on a parallel course. He did everything by the book, pausing every now and again to peer into shop windows to check his back the way his instructors had trained him at Gerrards Cross. He spent twenty minutes browsing through a bookstore and bought a Nester's *Street Guide to New York* and a map of Long Island before leaving. At West Forty-ninth Street he crossed over to the other side of the avenue and continued northward, still observing the procedures he'd been taught.

By the time he reached Radio City Music Hall, Abbott was reasonably certain that he was being followed. There were two of them: a lean, cadaverous-looking man in a green check topcoat and an equally tall but far more heavily built man who wore glasses and carried a briefcase in his left hand. He had first become aware of them before entering the bookstore and since then they had switched positions on several occasions. Ten minutes ago the man with the briefcase had been twenty yards or so ahead of him but now he had dropped back, changing places with the character in the green topcoat.

Abbott crossed the avenue for the second time at the next intersection, stopped briefly outside the Equitable Life Building, and then, doubling back on his tracks, entered the IND subway station at Fiftieth Street. Obtaining a token from the booth, he dropped it into the turnstile and made his way down to the southbound local platform. Any notion that he might have gotten it wrong, that there was really no cause for alarm, was dispelled a few moments after the train rumbled out of the tunnel and swept into the station. As he boarded the fourth car he saw the man with the briefcase double past to enter the car behind. Poking his head outside, Abbott noticed that the other man was still on the platform near the motorman's cab and guessed he was waiting until the last minute to make sure he didn't leave the train before it pulled out. *I'm the meat in the sandwich,* he thought, and sat down in the nearest seat. Then the doors closed and with a sudden jerk the train started to move forward.

He thought it would be a waste of time to speculate how, when, or why McNulty's associates were onto him. His first priority was to shake them off and once that aim had been achieved, he would have to find a bolt-hole and move out of the Taft Hotel. The various tactical moves that Winter had planned were no longer relevant because their opponents were not responding in the way he'd predicted. Other safeguards were needed now to ensure that Hedley could go it alone should he be taken out of the game. Some alternative means of communication was necessary because in the final extremity Hedley would have to know where he had deposited the Eisenhower material. A dead letter box? No, that was too insecure. A mailbox at an out-of-town address? That was more like it. It wouldn't be difficult to pick a suitable location; he had a map of Long Island in his coat pocket. As Abbott pulled it out, he looked up and, glancing to his right, saw that the man with the briefcase was standing by the communicating door, watching his every move.

"This is Forty-second Street." The nasal voice of the train conductor came through loud and clear over the microphone and he almost jumped out of his skin. "This station is Forty-second Street. The next stop is Thirty-fourth Street."

Abbott glanced at his wristwatch: 9:45. Hedley's plane had been delayed by fog at Gander but it should be landing at Idlewild any time now; that was the latest ETA BOAC had given him when he'd telephoned flight information from the hotel. Abbott frowned; he wasn't thinking straight. The ETA was only of academic interest to him; the essential point was that he should be waiting outside the pay phone in the drugstore on East Forty-ninth when Hedley called at 7:30. He had 9¾ hours then, 9¾ hours to slip the stalkers, find a bolt-hole, and set up an alternative means of communication. He would be pressed for time but it wasn't impossible and he had everything he needed: international driver's license, passport, and $875 in the money belt around his waist.

The train began to slow down and he braced himself, knowing they were approaching Thirty-fourth Street. There was a chance he could lose one of them at this stop if he was smart enough, if the man with the briefcase was caught on the hop. If, if, if; the permutations were limitless and there was always that unpredictable joker, the element of luck.

The train pulled into the station, the same nasal voice spoke through the microphone, and the doors slid open. Abbott sat there watching the passengers get in and out of the car while he waited for exactly the right moment to make his move. The doors started to close and he left his seat on the run, but his timing was all wrong and they slammed in his face before he ·was halfway there.

Abbott knew without looking around that the stalker in the next car was highly amused and the knowledge that he'd made a laughingstock of himself only increased his anger. No practical experience—that was his trouble. Oh, he was strong on theory all right, could tell other people how to do it, but come the moment and he couldn't put the teaching into practice. The head of steam blew off and his anger swiftly evaporated. By the time the train pulled into Twenty-third Street he was cool again and ready to go.

Abbott hit the platform and was running toward the exit before the doors were fully open. He took the steps two at a time, weaving this way and that to avoid bumping into the other passengers, the man in the green topcoat hard on his heels. Turning right outside the entrance, he legged it into the Avenue of the Americas and flagged down a passing cab. A *lucky break at last*, he thought, but as he told the cabdriver to take him to Penn Station, the lights went red, holding them long enough for his pursuers to wipe out the advantage he'd gained. Looking over his shoulder, Abbott saw them pile into a cab that was tucked in behind a bus in the adjoining lane.

They were sticking to him like leeches and he doubted if he could lose them in the main concourse of Penn Station. Opening up the street map, he searched for a suitable alternative.

"I've changed my mind," Abbott said. "Forget Penn Station. Take me to Macy's instead."

"Which entrance?"

"Any one will do," said Abbott. "I've just remembered that it's my wife's birthday tomorrow."

"Yeah?"

"There'll be hell to pay if I don't get her a present. You know how it is."

"I don't," said the cabdriver. "I'm not married. Thirty-fourth Street okay?"

"Sure."

Abbott paid off the cab and hurried into Macy's. At that hour of the morning the world's largest department store was not quite the seething mass of humanity he could have wished for, but there were enough shoppers around to make life difficult for his two shadows. Fifteen minutes later, having toured the second floor and switched elevators on the fifth, he slipped out through one of the employees' entrances as clean as a brand-new penny whistle.

From then on everything was more or less plain sailing. Taking a cab from Herald Square to the IRT subway station at Wall Street, he boarded a train for Utica Avenue on the Seventh Avenue line. Leaving the subway, he hired a Dodge sedan from a rental agency on Utica Avenue and headed east on Route 27. Forty-six miles and sixty-five minutes later, he reached Seaford. At five past two, having seen a local real estate agent and visited the post office, he set off on the return leg to Brooklyn. By five o'clock he had returned the Dodge to the rental agency and found himself a furnished apartment on nearby Union Street. He then had 2½ hours in which to move his baggage from the Taft Hotel to the rented apartment and make it back to the drugstore on East Forty-ninth Street.

New Yorkers called it the cocktail hour, but as far as Hedley could see there was precious little demand for anything as exotic as a dry martini, a white lady, a screwdriver, or a manhattan at the Shamrock Inn on Fifth Avenue. In an Irish bar it was expedient to drink only Irish whiskey, like all the other men who were standing shoulder to shoulder with one foot on the rail, necks craned and eyes fixed on the TV set mounted high on the back wall. As he watched with the others, a horizontal line appeared at the bottom of the picture and moved up the frame, neatly dissecting Eisenhower at the waist, chest, and head.

"That Eisenhower," said a voice down the bar from Hedley.

"He's going to walk it."

"It's not a one-horse race," said the bartender. "I think Adlai Stevenson will run him close."

"An egghead. Who wants an egghead for president?"

"Who wants a sick man in the White House?" The bartender jerked a thumb at the TV set above his head. "You hear that?" he challenged. "He's going into Walter Reed tomorrow."

"For a checkup," said the unidentified voice. "Ike will be out on Sunday, you'll see."

"If Eisenhower gets reelected," the bartender growled, "Nixon will be sitting in the Oval Office before his second term is up."

The argument died when the commercials replaced Eisenhower on the screen and a pretty blonde extolled the virtues of a General Electric refrigerator and reminded any husbands who might be watching that there were only fifty shopping days to Christmas. Automobiles, detergents, Kodak cameras, and Chesterfield cigarettes—one hard sell followed another in what seemed an endless catalogue of consumer products.

The commercials finally ended and the newscaster came back on the screen to introduce a film report from Budapest which opened with a shot of machine gun posts sited behind a line of trees in a small park and two bodies partially covered with the Hungarian national flag. *Rose Hill near the Boulevard of Martyrs*, Hedley thought, recognizing the locality, and then there was a swift change of scene to Hovarth Square and the barricades of burnt-out motor vehicles and overturned street-cars. The camera moved with bewildering speed, showing first a platoon of Soviet tanks drawn up in front of the glass-domed East Railway Station, then panning to the Hotel Astoria on the corner of Rakosi Street with a close-up of the shards of glass littering the pavement. Soviet troops fraternizing with Hungarian citizens in one part of the city and firing on them elsewhere in Budapest. Soviet troops fighting on the side of the AVH in the Eighth and Ninth districts and against them outside Parliament House.

"It sure is a goddamned mess," said the bartender.

154

You're right in more ways than one, Hedley thought, and swallowed the rest of his whiskey.

After leaving the Shamrock Inn, he walked north to Forty-ninth Street and, skirting the sunken garden in Rockefeller Center, entered the RCA Building. PLaza 3-2607: one of the two contact numbers Winter had impressed upon him the night they'd driven through South London, the one he was supposed to call first. At exactly 7:30, Hedley slipped into a phone booth near the cafeteria on the lower concourse and dialed the number. It rang twice and then, in a muffled voice, Abbott said, "2607, Four Square Laundry." Hedley closed his eyes. They were 3000 miles from home but some things hadn't changed; they were still using the same banal recognition code.

"Hello, Miles," he said. "Washed any dirty linen today?"

"No, I've been too busy looking out for myself." Abbott laughed uneasily. "I've had two rather ugly-looking characters on my tail."

"McNulty was certainly quick off the mark." Hedley frowned; that had to be the understatement of the week. Miles had been smuggled out of London almost forty-eight hours ago, but evidently McNulty had tumbled to it and a reception committee had been waiting for him at the airport.

"Too quick," said Abbott. "I have a nasty feeling they're not on the same side as McNulty. Anyway, I thought it best to move out of the Taft Hotel."

"What makes you think they haven't followed you to your new address?"

"Because I took damned good care to lose them before I checked out."

Checked out? Hedley wondered if he'd heard Miles correctly. "Don't tell me you returned to the hotel and settled your bill?" he said disbelievingly.

"Well, of course I did. I wanted them to think I'd left New York. Besides, I've got enough problems to cope with as it is without having to stay one jump ahead of the police."

Abbott wasn't a jump ahead of anybody. Once they'd lost him, the opposition would have doubled back to the hotel because that was their only lead. It was the kind of long shot that usually failed nine times out of ten, but Miles had been stupid enough to give them a second chance.

"I've been looking at a property in Seaford," Abbott said abruptly.

"Where?"

"Seaford, over on Long Island. I thought an out-of-town address might come in handy." Abbott paused. Then in a somewhat breathless voice and talking rapidly as though it was a matter of extreme urgency, he went on, "If by any chance you don't hear from me for a while, call at the local post office and ask if they have any mail for you. Your box number is 2077. I rented a house on Division Avenue to make it look right."

"What did you tell the real estate people?"

"I didn't have to tell them anything," Abbott said peevishly. "It's a summer place and the house stands empty for eight months of the year. With the off season only a few weeks old, they were only too glad to rent it out for three months. The lease is in your name and I paid a month in advance, which was another reason why they didn't ask me any questions. The house is called Two Acres. Remember that—it could be important."

"Is there anything else I should know, Miles?"

"Not really. I'm having trouble running Emsden to ground, but with any luck I may have some news for you tomorrow night."

"Don't rush it," said Hedley. "Take your time."

"Time is one thing we don't have," said Abbott.

"To hell with the schedule," Hedley said. "It's crazy to take unnecessary risks."

"Thanks for the advice." Abbott laughed again but there was no mirth in it and his mood swiftly changed, becoming somber in a matter of seconds. "Don't worry," he said grimly, "I'll remember to look over my shoulder."

"You do that, Miles." Hedley bit his lip. He didn't want to alarm Abbott but it was unlikely that the change of address had fooled the opposition. He thought Miles should forget Emsden and find another bolt-hole, but before he could put his thoughts into words, there was a sharp click followed by a continuous *burring* noise and he realized that Abbott had hung up on him. Replacing the phone, he left the booth and walked straight into a three-man reception committee.

Two of them were standing practically shoulder to shoulder and were dressed alike in dark blue raincoats. The third man was wearing a single-breasted herringbone that looked as if it had been made by an English tailor.

"Good evening, Mr. Hedley," said the man in the herringbone suit. "My name is Kaplin."

"Your face seems vaguely familiar." Hedley stared at him. "And you know my name. Have we met somewhere before?"

"You may have seen me on the BOAC flight last night."

Hedley nodded. He could place him now; Kaplin had been sitting five rows back and across the aisle from him. "We weren't introduced," he said coldly. "So how do you know my name?"

"I make a point of knowing our competitors." Kaplin smiled. "You see, we're in the same line of business."

"I'm a press correspondent," said Hedley.

"And I'm a PR man, but that docsn't necessarily mean we're on opposite sides of the fence. In fact, it's quite possible that my company will make a very generous offer for your story, Mr. Hedley."

"What story?"

"The one that involves Telegraph Cottage, Wyecroft Farm, and La Bouée Hotel."

Hedley didn't like it. Everything was happening a lot faster than Winter had predicted. McNulty's people were supposed to approach him after he'd seen Emsden, not before.

"You'd be well advised to do business with me." Kaplin pointed to the two men standing opposite him. "Mr. Nolan and Mr. Quirk are employed by a rival concern and they're unlikely to offer you such a good deal."

Hedley glanced in their direction. Nolan and Quirk were like two peas in a pod. They were roughly the same age, height, and build and he suddenly had a feeling that their dark blue raincoats had been issued free of charge.

"They're with the N.Y.P.D.," Kaplin added gratuitously.

"I'll take your word for it."

"You don't have to," Nolan said, producing his shield.

"All right," said Hedley, "I'm convinced. Where do we go from here?"

"Downtown," said Kaplin. "There's someone there who wants to talk to you."

Downtown turned out to be a twenty-minute ride in a Cadillac to Nassau Street and the offices of the Zenith Technical Corporation on the fourth floor of the Potter Building, where Hedley was left to cool his heels in a stuffy reception room.

No one came near him for the best part of an hour, but that didn't surprise him. Familiar with the techniques of interrogation, Hedley knew that Kaplin would be watching him through some spy-hole to see how he was reacting to the psychological pressure. In what was essentially a contest of wills, he had only one line of defense and, making himself as comfortable as possible, he closed his eyes and went to sleep. At half past nine, Kaplin threw in the sponge; shaking Hedley awake, he hustled him into the boardroom at the far end of the corridor.

Although a front organization for the CIA, the Zenith Technical Corporation had all the trappings of a legitimate business enterprise. The boardroom was furnished in style with a long mahogany table, soft upholstered chairs, a fitted carpet, and velvet drapes in the windows. According to the New York Stock Exchange, the major stockholder and president of the corporation was Walter H. Zenith, Jr., but on this occasion, sitting in his chair at the head of the table was Janet Roscoe.

Hedley said, "Hello, Miss Roscoe. It's a small world, isn't it?"

"Sometimes it can be too small." She pointed to a chair halfway down the table. "Sit down, Mr. Hedley." Her voice was cold and hard. "This won't take long."

"Good." Hedley smiled, ignoring the frosty reception. "I'm

sure we can reach an amicable agreement. Perhaps it would save time if I put my cards on the table?"

"You don't have any."

Hedley shook his head. "I'm disappointed in you, Miss Roscoe. I thought you were an intelligent young woman."

"If anyone is being stupid, it's you." Janet leaned forward, her elbows on the table, hands clasped together, the index fingers pointing upward like a church steeple. "Any deal we make is going to be on our terms."

"I'm sure you're not joking," said Hedley, "so you must be a Democrat. I mean, there has to be some reason why you don't want to see Eisenhower reelected."

"I know what you have in mind, but it isn't going to work." Janet moved her wrists and leveled a pair of accusing fingers at his chest. "You see, you're in very serious trouble with our Customs people."

"Surprise, surprise," he said ironically.

"You'd better believe it," said Kaplin. "They opened a package belonging to you—and guess what? They found it contained $250,000 worth of uncut heroin. You want to hear the rest of the story?"

"No," said Hedley, "but I have a feeling you're going to tell me anyway."

"Damn right I am. You took delivery of the stuff when you were in Cannes and sent it over here in a diplomatic pouch belonging to the British Information Service. To Await Collection: that's what the docket says, and it's in your handwriting."

They had gone one better than Winter, and with all the resources at their disposal he knew they could make the charge stick. Nolan and Quirk would back them up and swear they'd heard him talking to a buyer. If necessary, they could always fake the telephone conversation.

"You can forget Winter," Janet said coolly. "He won't lift a finger to help you. He can't afford to."

"It would seem we've reached an impasse," said Hedley. "You can lock me up and throw away the key but that won't solve anything. We can still flush Eisenhower down the drain."

"You deliver those letters to me and I'll put you on a plane to England. That's the deal, Mr. Hedley."

"And a very attractive proposition it is too."

"I'm glad you think so," said Janet.

"There's only one snag. I don't have the letters."

"We already know that," said Kaplin. "We went through your luggage at the airport."

"So?"

"So that leaves Miles Abbott," said Janet. "You phoned him once, you can phone him again."

Pure guesswork, he thought, and wished he was wrong because it meant that Miles was in real trouble. At least two men were sitting on his tail and clearly they weren't taking their orders from the Americans. Had they been working for the CIA, then both he and Miles would now be facing Janet Roscoe across the table.

"I'm supposed to call him at 7:30 tomorrow night," Hedley said slowly. "He'll be in a phone booth somewhere in the area of Madison Avenue. The number is 576-8900. I imagine you can get the exact location from the telephone company."

"You don't have to deliver Abbott," Kaplin said contemptuously. "Just the letters."

"They're indivisible," Hedley snapped. "The others are aware of that even if you aren't."

"What others?" said Janet. "Who are you talking about?"

"Two men who don't belong to your organization. Miles is convinced he has shaken them off, but I think he's wrong. I don't know what they're planning to do but if they get to him first, I've a hunch we'll both lose out. That's why I think you should start looking for him now. Miles checked out of the Taft sometime today; where he's gone to is anyone's guess."

It was impossible to tell whether Janet believed him or not. Her face gave nothing away but the small frown on her forehead and the way her pink tongue was exploring the bottom lip suggested that at least she was thinking about it.

"What do you think, Leo?" she asked presently.

"I don't buy Hedley's story," said Kaplin. "It's misinforma-

160

tion. I don't know what his angle is but we've no reason to trust him."

Offhand, Hedley couldn't think of a single reason why they should believe his story either, but somehow he had to convince them that a third party was now involved. He owed that much to Miles.

"There must have been a leak," Hedley said forcefully. "Some Arab sympathizer in the SIS must have tipped off the Egyptians and they decided to do something about it."

"Don't pay any attention to him, Jan. The Egyptians don't have the capacity to do anything over here."

"They have friends," said Hedley. "I think the KGB would be prepared to help them out. The Russians have a two-fold aim: they want to keep their toehold in the Middle East and crush the Hungarian uprising. Right now it's in their interest to insure that most of Eisenhower's energies are directed against us and the French."

"It's a familiar argument," said Janet.

Her voice was neutral but he knew what she was thinking. The question-and-answer session at Burnham House had been a dismal failure because McNulty had known all along that Winter was trying to influence American policy, to switch their attention from Suez to Hungary.

"You're in the driver's seat, Jan," Kaplin said quietly. "How do you want to play it?"

The small frown appeared again but not for long. "Nothing has changed," she said in a decisive voice. "We'll keep Hedley under wraps at the house on West Fifty-sixth Street. Take him back to the Algonquin, collect his luggage, and settle the bill."

"I think you're making a big mistake," said Hedley, but they were past listening to him.

Abbott left the IRT subway at Utica Avenue in Brooklyn and started walking toward Union Street. It had been a long day, but although he hadn't been able to do anything about Emsden, it hadn't been an entirely unproductive one. Hedley had established contact and he'd warned him about the gate-crashers, and if things did really go sour, at least the letters were safe now that he'd mailed the house key to the box number in Seaford.

Hedley appeared to think he'd failed to shake off the two men tailing him, but there had been no sign of them when he left the drugstore on East Forty-ninth. No one had followed him to Larré's French restaurant on West Fifty-sixth Street, and God knows he'd taken every precaution since then: a cab from Larré's to Grand Central, another to the Empire State Building, and a third to the Fourteenth Street station on the IRT's Seventh Avenue Line. Hands thrust deep into the pockets of his overcoat, the collar turned up to protect his ears against the chill wind, Abbott turned left on Union Street and headed toward Lincoln Terrace Park.

The black Oldsmobile was parked in the shadow midway between the two nearest streetlights and roughly fifty yards up the road from the apartment house where Abbott was staying. Abbott assumed the Olds, like the Plymouth that was parked in front of it, belonged to one of the residents, and it wasn't until both nearside doors opened simultaneously and two men scrambled out of the sedan that he knew different. As he opened his mouth to shout for help, a lead-filled sock crunched into his skull and he plunged headfirst into a deep black hole.

14.

Abbott came to, shivering violently as though he had a severe bout of malaria. His body was numb with cold, his head throbbed, and his limbs seemed paralyzed. He tried to move his arms and legs but nothing happened, and then it dawned on him that he was tied to a chair. The cords were biting into his wrists and ankles, and his elbows were drawn together behind his back so that his shoulders were braced. The reason why he was frozen to the bone was not hard to discover either: glancing down, he saw that he had been stripped to the waist and his socks and shoes removed.

He could hear a recurrent slapping noise and there was a fusty smell in the air which reminded him of something. Mushrooms? Rotting timbers? Abbott peered about him, but apart from a gray chink of light above his head, he could see very little in the prevailing gloom. A wooden building somewhere on the waterfront? His feet were certainly resting on bare boards and the movement of water would account for the slapping noise.

A hoarse voice behind him said, "Good morning, Mr. Abbott. I trust you slept well?"

Morning? How long had he been unconscious then? Six, eight hours? Surely a knock on the head couldn't have put him to sleep that long. His mouth was dry and his tongue felt like it was coated with paste. He'd been drugged; that was the answer.

"Could I have a drink of water?" he croaked.

"You hear that, Zabrowski? He's thirsty."

"We'll have to do something about that, won't we, Panov?"

The second voice was somewhere to his front, and then a beam of light played on his face and a burly figure came toward him out of the darkness. Squinting against the glare, Abbott saw that he was wearing glasses and knew it was the man he'd seen yesterday carrying a briefcase.

"Maybe; then again, maybe not," said Panov. "It depends how cooperative he is."

Their accents were American, their names either Russian or Polish. Somebody had once told him there were 2 million Americans of Russian descent living in and around New York City, a singularly useless piece of information like many of the other facts and figures he'd absorbed over the years. They had disclosed their identities, that was the really significant point he should be thinking about because the breach of security had been quite deliberate. They wanted him to know who they were, and he didn't like the implication one little bit.

"Somehow I don't think our friend is the cooperative type."

"Try him," said Panov.

"How about it, Miles?" Zabrowski moved closer still and aimed the flashlight's beam directly into his eyes. "You want to tell us where you've hidden those letters?"

"What letters?" he asked.

"You see?" Zabrowski said. "I told you he wasn't the cooperative type."

"Oh, I don't know," said Panov. "I think he can be persuaded to change his mind."

A pair of callused hands descended on his bare shoulders and the chair began to tilt over backward until it was teetering on the rear legs. Then Panov released his grip and stepped out of the way so the chair overbalanced and crashed to the floor. The fall jarred every bone in Abbott's spine and reopened the

164

wound in his skull made by the lead-filled sock.

"About these letters," Zabrowski said casually. "Why don't you tell us where they are and save yourself a lot of grief?"

"If you should be unfortunate enough to fall into the hands of the Gestapo, play for time, prolong the moment of agony for as long as you can." Abbott could hear the instructor's voice now, crisp and confident as he addressed the class of SOE agents under training at Wanborough Manor. The advice might be fifteen years old but it was equally relevant today.

"I don't know what you're talking about," he said slowly.

"Wouldn't you just know it?" said Panov. "We've got ourselves a hero."

"So it would seem," Zabrowski said in a voice that conveyed disgust.

Panov walked past him and disappeared into the gloom beyond the beam of light that continued to play on his face as he lay on the floor. A few moments later, the tall thin man with the cadaverous face returned with a bucket of water, a ladle, and a towel.

"You know something?" Abbott managed a faint smile. "I'm no longer thirsty."

"We think you are." Panov crouched beside him and draped the towel over his face. "And we know best, don't we, Zabrowski?"

"You bet we do," Zabrowski said, and whinnied like a horse.

Abbott heard the ladle dip into the bucket and even though he knew what to expect, the sudden douche of water made him panic. The damp towel molded to his face like a linen shroud and he found it difficult to breathe. Another ladleful emptied over the towel and the water trickled into his nose and mouth. In mounting desperation he twisted his head from side to side in a vain attempt to dislodge the towel. Three ladlefuls and he was coughing and spluttering; four, and there was a loud rushing noise in both ears which reduced the repetitive questions to a mere whisper.

"You will face the most rigorous forms of interrogation and

at times you will be convinced you're dying. But always remember this: the Gestapo won't kill you before they've squeezed you dry. It is, I admit, a very small crumb of comfort, but it's the best I can offer, so hang onto it." The way he'd talked, you'd have thought the instructor had been through the mill himself, but the words of wisdom were secondhand and the bastard was wrong. The bastard was wrong because he was drowning, the waters closing above his head and taking him down, down into the deep.

The darkness exploded into light with a shaft of excruciating pain that made Abbott rear back in the chair and moan in agony as the cigarette end burned into his neck. Within a matter of seconds the moan was overtaken by a paroxysm of coughing that racked his lungs and brought up sputum. The bile spurted from his open mouth and ran down his chest, but after a while the retching stopped and he began to breathe almost normally once more. Then, with awareness, came the realization that he was sitting bolt upright, that the chair was standing on all four legs.

Zabrowski said, "Why be difficult, Miles? We know you've got the letters."

"There will come a time," the instructor had said, *"when you will feel you're incapable of further resistance. That's perfectly understandable. The body can only take so much punishment before the spirit breaks, but a lot of people are depending on you, and you must hold out until news of your arrest by the Gestapo filters through to the Resistance. They will need time to warn the other members of your cell and arrange for them to go into hiding. From operational research we know this can take up to three days from the time you're arrested."*

Zabrowski placed a hand under Abbott's chin and raised his head. "I'm talking to you, Miles."

"Yes."

"So why don't you answer me?"

"Three days, that's your aim in life. To achieve it, you must gain some respite from the rigorous methods of interrogation

166

used by the Gestapo. We therefore recommend that you should feed them some information. Give the interrogators a few tidbits to be going on with, information that can't hurt your friends."

"You know about the letters then," Abbott said in a dull, listless voice.

"Well, what do you know?" said Panov "I do believe we're getting somewhere at last."

"The letters were stolen from Kay Summersby," Abbott went on. "At least, that's the story I've given Emsden."

"Emsden?" Zabrowski repeated. "Who's he?"

"A muckraker. He digs up dirt for a gossip columnist."

"String them along," the instructor had advised. "Lead them down every byway you can. They will tumble to it in the end, but you will have gained a valuable respite."

"Anyway, I sent him a sweetener before you picked me up."

"He's lying."

The voice was hard and came from the dark. The sudden realization that a third man was sitting in on the interrogation gave Abbott a nasty jolt and for some moments he was thrown completely off balance.

"What have you got to say to that?" Panov demanded.

"I arrived in New York late on Wednesday evening . . . " Abbott paused and licked his lips. "The following morning I contacted Walter Emsden . . . "

"He's lying," said the third man.

"Listen," Abbott said desperately, "Emsden has an office in the J. C. Penney Building . . . "

"He's still lying."

"Yeah, I think so too," said Panov. Bending down, he grabbed both front legs and upended the chair.

"Whatever you do, don't let them see you're bluffing." The instructor's words echoed mockingly in his ears as Panov arranged the sodden towel over his face and reached for the ladle.

Beyond Abbott's dark and terrifying world, the sun began its slow ascent above the horizon. In the half light of daybreak, the mud flats of Gravesend Bay and the old wooden paddlewheeler rotting by the jetty were endowed with a certain rustic charm.

The brownstone house on West Fifty-sixth Street was divided into three separate apartments, each roughly the same size and containing an entrance hall, cloakroom, two bedrooms, a living room, a kitchenette, and a bathroom. The first- and third-floor apartments were occupied by two executives of the Zenith Technical Corporation whose wives, it just so happened, were also on the company's payroll. The second floor was reserved for guests, a euphemism for people who, like Hedley, were often detained against their will.

In official jargon he was a detainee, which meant that, amongst other things, he'd had to surrender his passport to Kaplin along with the residue of the $850 Winter had allowed him for expenses. Although Hedley was free to rove the apartment during the day, Kaplin had also confiscated his jacket, shoes, and overcoat, a precaution that was intended to discourage any thoughts of escape. The clear blue sky and bright sunlight made the weather look deceptively mild outside, but the temperature was in the low thirties and he didn't need Quirk to remind him that he'd look pretty stupid wandering about in shirtsleeves and stockinged feet.

"I wouldn't try it if I were you," Janet Roscoe said in a level voice.

Hedley turned his back to the window. "Try what?" he asked.

"Jumping out of the window. It's a long drop to the sidewalk."

"Why discourage him, Jan?" Quirk stretched both arms above his head and yawned loudly. "With any luck, he'd break both legs and end up in the hospital. Then some nurse could do the baby-sitting instead of us."

Hedley said, "You know something, Miss Roscoe? I think your policemen are just wonderful."

"Tell him, Jan," Quirk said, smiling broadly. "Tell the man how we took him for a ride."

168

"You're not a policeman?"

"No."

"And Nolan, is he a phony too?"

"Don't build up your hopes," Kaplin cut in swiftly. "Nolan is genuine; he'll lay it on you any time we give the word."

Hedley glanced around the living room. It wasn't his intention to cut and run, but it was obvious they weren't taking any chances. Kaplin was between him and the door to the hallway while Quirk, for all that he was lounging in an armchair, was in a position to block the way to the kitchen-diner and the fire escape at the back. Janet Roscoe occupied a corner seat on the couch, a telephone at her elbow on the occasional table in case she needed to summon help.

"I won't give you any trouble," he said. "I know the score, Kaplin. You spelled it out to me in some detail last night."

"Then why are you so restless?" Janet asked quietly.

"I'm worried about Miles. We should be out looking for him instead of sitting here waiting to make that phone call at 7:30."

"Here we go again." Kaplin sighed. "You never give up, do you, Hedley?"

"Look, I'll make a deal with you. Call the Taft Hotel and ask the desk clerk if he remembers anyone inquiring after Abbott. If the answer's no, you won't hear another word from me. That's a promise."

"I suppose we could ask Nolan to check it out." Kaplin looked to Janet Roscoe for confirmation. "If nothing else, it may keep Hedley quiet for a while."

"There is that possibility, Leo."

"Yes. Well, I'll use the phone in the kitchen; it's more private." Kaplin eyed Hedley for a moment and then locked the door to the hallway and pocketed the key. "I don't want to put temptation in your way," he said cheerfully.

In Kaplin's shoes, Hedley would have done the same, but nevertheless it still rankled and the American's skepticism raised fresh doubts in his mind. What if he was wrong and Miles had lost his tail? Neither possibility bore thinking about.

"A penny for your thoughts," said Janet.

"I doubt if you would think they were worth it, Miss Roscoe."

"Okay, let's try another tack. Do you play chess?"

"A little and badly," he said.

"Never mind. It'll help to pass the time." Janet got up and walked across the room to crouch in front of one of the built-in cupboards under the bookshelves that spanned the length of one wall. "We'll need a table," she said briskly.

"Yes, of course." There was only one table that Hedley could see, the small one by the couch. "We seem to be a bit limited," he said. "What do you want me to do with the telephone?"

"Put it over there," Janet said, pointing to a small writing desk in the corner.

Quirk made a face, muttered something unintelligible under his breath and, launching himself from the armchair, went into the kitchen. Returning with two cans of beer, he switched on the television and sat down again.

"You two intellectuals don't mind if I watch TV, do you?" he asked.

"Not if you keep the volume down," Janet said.

"Affects the concentration, does it?"

As far as Hedley was concerned, any background noise would have a minimal effect on his concentration compared with Janet Roscoe. "A pretty little thing" in Deakin's opinion, but beauty lay in the eye of the beholder and from the moment he'd first seen her at Burnham House he'd thought she was easily the most attactive woman he'd ever met. Tall, slender, graceful, a good figure, dark brown glossy hair, and green eyes —the physical attributes were obvious enough but there were other qualities that he found harder to define. There was no apposite phrase he could think of to describe adequately the attraction she held for him, except a conviction that there was no one quite like her. He just wished they weren't on opposite sides of the fence, particularly now that she'd begun to thaw toward him.

"It's your move," Janet said.

Hedley looked at the board, saw that she'd opened the game by moving a pawn to King four, and followed suit. Responding, Janet began to attack from the center to such purpose that he was forced onto the defensive. Capturing two pawns, a knight, and the Queen's bishop in rapid succession, she maneuvered him into fighting a losing battle where he was obliged to sacrifice one piece after another in order to protect his King.

"You're too good for me," he said.

"Well, you're probably out of practice and I learned my game from a master."

"Who was that?"

"My father. He used to say it was good training for a lawyer. I don't know if there's any truth in that proposition, but he was pretty good in court. There was a time when I wanted to follow in his footsteps, but I changed my mind shortly after graduating from Columbia University Law School." Janet frowned. "No, that's not strictly accurate; I took a pace sideways and went off in another direction."

Although there had been no shortage of opportunities in New York, a desire to make her own way in life had led Janet to Washington and a job in the Justice Department. At a time when the CIA was still expanding to meet the demands of the cold war, it was almost inevitable that one of their recruiters should approach her.

"He made the job sound very interesting, but I guess that wasn't the only selling point. It's hard to explain but I felt I owed something to my country. Maybe that sounds a little corny, but I was brought up in a home where patriotism wasn't a dirty word. Anyway, when he started waving the flag at me, I joined up and signed on the dotted line."

No one had waved a flag at Hedley while he was up at Oxford, the difference being that British Intelligence had always preferred to do their recruiting through the old boy network. Just how he had come to their notice was still something of a mystery, but he suspected his French tutor had set the ball rolling with a few chosen words in the right ear. As a wartime member of the Special Operations Executive, he was certainly well qualified to be a talent spotter for the SIS.

"Checkmate," she said and clapped her hands.

"Same thing applies to the Russians." Quirk waved a beer can in the general direction of the TV screen. "They don't seem to know which way to turn. There are liberation committees springing up all over Hungary. I can't pronounce the names of the places, but they've kicked the Soviets out of a couple of towns, that I do know." Quirk raised the can to his lips for a mouthful of beer and then wiped his lips with the back of his hand. "Ever hear of a guy called Attila something-or-other?" he asked.

"Do you mean Attila Szigetti?" said Hedley.

"Yeah, that's the guy. He's been telling Imre Nagy that the people have no confidence in his government."

"That should do wonders for Nagy's confidence," Hedley said.

"Nagy is out of step with the rest of the country. 'The people have given their judgment and the Soviet troops should be sent home.' That's what this Szigetti said."

Hedley recalled the card index on Szigetti that had been part of his required reading before he was posted to Budapest. Apart from giving his date and place of birth, it had merely recorded that he'd been a deputy in the first postwar Hungarian government. A huge commanding man with bristling red mustaches, he was, according to the SIS report, a fiery orator with a strong personal following in the provinces.

"People like him are going to push Nagy too far."

"He needs pushing," said Quirk. "A neutral Hungary—that's what the people are demanding and that's what he has to deliver."

"A neutral Hungary? You mean they want to leave the Warsaw Pact?"

"They sure do." Quirk beamed happily. "Isn't that just dandy for us?"

"It's unrealistic. The best you can hope for is that the Russians will agree to withdraw their troops. Personally, I'd settle for that."

"Yeah, well, you would."

"Nagy is walking a tightrope," Hedley said tersely. "Provided he's allowed to play it his way, he may just get a settlement on the lines Gomulka achieved for Poland. If a bunch of extremists join the high-wire act, he won't stand a chance. Khrushchev will break his spine."

It occurred to Hedley that he had a lot in common with the people who were pushing Nagy over the brink. Faced with a well-nigh insuperable problem, Winter had resorted to intimidation, the none-too-gentle art of persuasion by other means. In an era where labels were in vogue, "extremist" was as good a description as any for Winter, Abbott, and himself.

"You know something?" he said to Janet. "I think I've just been talking to myself."

The phone rang in the kitchen, pealing just twice before Kaplin answered its strident summons. The resultant conversation was brief and largely one-sided. All he heard from Kaplin was a series of monosyllabic grunts, but no extrasensory perception was required to know what had passed between him and Nolan. One look at the sardonic expression on his narrow face gave him the answer.

"Nolan drew a blank, then?"

"Of course he did." Kaplin scowled. "I knew all along it was a diversion."

"I don't agree," Janet said firmly.

He was no longer alone, but even though Janet had sided with him on this occasion, the odds were still adverse and nothing had changed. Eight valuable hours would still be wasted because all the facts supported Kaplin's contention that Miles had simply gone to ground, and he didn't have one solid piece of evidence to refute it. Kaplin would probably have second thoughts when the 7:30 call went unanswered, but by then it could well be too late. A gut feeling told him that time was fast running out for Miles.

15.

The bottom half of the door had broken off and beyond it Abbott could just see part of a catwalk and a junk-yard of rusty machinery which he assumed had once been the engine room. The chink of light that he'd previously observed above his head had first grown brighter, then dimmed again as the sun moved from east to west. At a guess, he thought the time was now roughly about four o'clock in the afternoon, which meant that, at the very least, it would be another 3½ hours before Hedley realized he was missing. Whether he would then be able to trace him was highly debatable. He wished he'd thought to give Hedley his new address. That would have been a starting point, but as it was, only Panov and Zabrowski knew about the apartment on Union Street.

The box number in Seaford was the one ace he had up his sleeve. In the absence of any other lead, Hedley would recall that he'd rented a house on Division Avenue and would go to the local post office to see if there was any mail waiting for him. The note he'd posted yesterday would tell him where the Eisen-hower letters had been hidden, and once they were in his possession there was no reason why he shouldn't tell Panov and Zabrowski everything they wanted to know. There was, however, one big snag: tomorrow was Sunday and the post office would be closed.

The instructor had said, "Three days, that's your aim in life," and it seemed he wasn't so far out even though the circumstances were wholly different. It was strange that this yardstick from yesteryear should apply to him, but by the time the post office was open for business again on Monday morning, he would have spent more than 2½ days in captivity.

Abbott clenched his hands, digging the fingernails into the palms. Monday was still forty-two hours away and he wasn't sure he could hold out that long. How many times had he almost drowned up to now? Five, or was it six? The number of burns inflicted with a lighted cigarette on his chest and neck suggested that it was the latter. "*Lead them down every byway you can. They will tumble to it in the end but you will have gained a valuable respite.*" The instructor's words again, but his advice had proved to be a load of bullshit. Panov, Zabrowski, and the third man weren't interested in Emsden, and as for the valuable respite, he doubted if he'd gained more than two hours so far.

"*Try to harbor your strength and snatch every moment of rest you can between sessions. Remember this: a tired man can't think straight and you'll need to have your wits about you to stay the course.*" There was another piece of advice from the past that had been found wanting. Perhaps the recommendations would begin to have some validity when he reached the stage of exhaustion where he was no longer conscious of the pain from his swollen wrists and ankles? From the low murmur of voices in the engine room and the sound of footsteps on the catwalk, it appeared he would soon know the answer to that proposition. Sick with apprehension, Abbott lowered his head and sagged in the chair, trying to give the impression that he was still unconscious. Then the key turned in the lock and the door opened inward.

Zabrowski said, "Oh, come on, Miles, surely you can do better than that?"

175

"I think he's cold," said Panov. "Shall we warm him up?"

A match flared and suddenly Abbott felt its heat close to his face. The flame singed his left eyebrow and burned a strand of hair, and jerking his head up, he reared back in the chair.

"That's one trick that never fails," Zabrowski observed casually.

Panov dropped the match onto the floor and stepped on it. Moving behind Abbott, he untied and removed the gag from his mouth. "It's time for another friendly talk," he said softly. "You want a drink of water before we start?"

"I'd sooner have a whiskey."

"You hear that?" said Panov. "Now we've got ourselves a joker."

"Like Hedley." Zabrowski leaned against the wooden partition, arms folded across his chest, relaxed and utterly sure of himself. "He's the other joker in the pack, isn't he, Miles?"

Abbott supposed the disclosure was intended to come like a thunderbolt out of the blue, but it had misfired because nothing Zabrowski said could surprise him anymore. That somebody had blown the whistle on the operation had been evident from the moment they had started to interrogate him. Given that premise, he would need to discover just how much they did know and then take it from there.

"The ace of trumps would be more accurate," he said.

"Don't kid yourself, Miles, he'll never find you."

"You're on the wrong track. Hedley won't come looking for me; that's not his job. He'll go straight to Emsden."

"Emsden again." Zabrowski clucked his tongue. "I'm tired of hearing his name."

"So am I," said Panov. "You think we should teach Miles a lesson?"

"He's certainly asking for one."

"For God's sake," Abbott said hoarsely, "I'm telling you the truth. Emsden is involved. We're using him to turn the screw on Eisenhower. With the election campaign about to enter the final week, he can't afford a major scandal at this stage of the race. Perhaps you find it hard to believe that a bunch of love letters could ruin his hopes for a second term in the White House?"

"Convince me."

Abbott hesitated. Either Zabrowski was testing him or else the unknown source in Whitehall hadn't passed on the full story. Whatever the reason behind the invitation, it was a golden opportunity to waste time and no harm would be done if he disclosed the basic concept. As long as the letters were safe, there was no way they could sabotage the operation.

"I'm waiting, Miles."

"I'm sorry—it's not an easy thing to explain." Abbott licked his lips and a dribble of saliva trickled from the corner of his mouth. "For what it's worth, we believe the majority of American voters expect their leaders to be above reproach. It's all right for Mr. Average Citizen to fool around but not the man who aspires to the highest office in the land. The way most people see it, the president must be incorruptible, a man of honor, integrity and sound judgment. So, if the Kay Summersby affair were to receive widespread publicity, a lot of people might well conclude that Eisenhower was conspicuously lacking in these qualities. Moreover, all the rumors circulating before the Republican Convention of '52 would be dragged out again and it would look as though there had been a deliberate cover-up."

"This Walter Emsden," Zabrowski said thoughtfully. "What prompted the SIS to choose him?"

"I've already told you: he's a muckraker."

Of all the possible candidates, Emsden had emerged as the front-runner. His track record showed that in the pursuit of making a fast buck he had no scruples whatever. The more sensational the story the better he liked it, and it didn't matter to him who got hurt in the process.

"I don't know how many libel suits have been filed against him, but either they've been settled out of court or else the proceedings have been dropped."

"A smooth operator," said Panov.

"He's all of that."

"And maybe he's just smart enough to question why an Englishman should want to supply him with the gossip story of the year."

"Hedley's also a journalist."

"What am I supposed to read into that?" Zabrowski asked.

"Well, knowing Hedley, he won't find it difficult to persuade Emsden that they're two of a kind. He'll tell him the story won't arouse any interest in England unless it's headline news in America. That's why he's prepared to give him the first bite at the cherry—for a consideration, of course, like a forty-sixty split in Emsden's favor."

Abbott paused to clear his throat. If he continued in the same vein, Zabrowski was bound to ask what evidence Hedley could produce to support his claim, and then Panov would lean on him again. To postpone that inevitable moment for as long as possible, it was vital he steered the conversation in a safer direction.

"Of course," he said, "we're counting on both the CIA and the State Department to intervene long before the deal is concluded."

"You think they'll offer to buy Hedley off?"

"It's in their interests to do so. After all, the asking price is not unreasonable. All we want from Eisenhower and Dulles is the right to settle the Suez dispute in our own way. There's also the American nuclear umbrella; we'd like to shelter under that should Khrushchev start to rattle his saber."

"Those objectives seem modest enough to me." Zabrowski smiled. "Given the means, Hedley might even have pulled it off."

"He still can," Abbott said vehemently. "I've set everything up for him and there's nothing you can do about it."

"He's bluffing," said Panov.

"You're wrong. I saw Emsden's secretary on Thursday and she gave me his address. He's spending this weekend in Hyannisport. That's how I was able to send him the registration slip from La Bouée."

"La Bouée?"

"It's a small hotel about ten miles northwest of Cannes. We made it look as though Eisenhower and Kay Summersby spent a night there in September '51. The reservation is for Mr. and Mrs. Ralph Summercorn of Columbus, Ohio, but Emsden is certain to recognize the signature."

"When he gets your letter," Zabrowski said.

"Yes."

"So what address did you mail it to in Hyannisport?"

The diversion had bought a little time, but it had also led him into a blind alley and there was no sidestepping the question. Emsden might be the worst kind of muckraker, but in this instance he was an innocent party and would have to be protected, and that wasn't going to be easy. A gossip columnist had to keep his ear to the ground at all times and he remembered Emsden's secretary telling him that her employer had an answering service so that his informants could either leave a message or know where to reach him after office hours.

"You must be looking for trouble," said Abbott. "Tangling with Emsden is just about the most stupid thing you can do."

"You're beginning to try my patience, Miles."

It happened fast, so fast that Abbott didn't have time to cry out. Ramming the gag into his mouth, Panov began to twist the little finger of his right hand, bending it farther and farther back until the bone snapped out of its socket. The pain was excruciating and when at last it began to subside and the gag was removed from his mouth, a small voice inside his head persuaded him that Emsden was not worth dying for.

"How about it, Miles?" Zabrowski asked softly. "Do I get the address?"

Abbott nodded. In a hoarse whisper, he said, "Emsden has a cottage on Chatham Road. It's called Seaview."

"Good. You'll find it pays to be cooperative."

"I don't know," said Panov. "He could be lying."

"I don't think so," said Zabrowski. "But we can soon check it out."

"You think?" Panov sounded dubious.

"I don't see why it should be a problem." Zabrowski reached

behind him and opened the door. "You stay here and keep an eye on our friend while I talk to the head man."

"Make it short," said Panov. "I don't want to be here all night."

The break was an unexpected bonus, one that Abbott hadn't grafted for. The head man was obviously the unseen figure who'd sat in on the preliminary interrogation and he just hoped the bastard wasn't readily available.

The minutes ticked away and he slumped in the chair listening to the sea lapping against the hull as the shaft of light above his head grew dimmer. For a while it began to look as if the respite would last until the 7:30 deadline with Hedley, but then Zabrowski returned and Abbott knew that his luck had finally run out.

"I make it exactly 7:30." Kaplin placed the telephone in front of Hedley. "You want to call Miles Abbott?"

Quirk and Nolan were waiting near the phone booth at 200 Madison Avenue. If everything went according to plan, Kaplin would raise them on the portable field radio when Miles answered his call and they would then move in and grab him. In theory the trap was foolproof, but Hedley knew it would be a different story when the time came to spring it.

"Don't hold your breath," he said.

"What's that supposed to mean?" Kaplin asked.

"It means I don't expect Miles to be there." Lifting the receiver, Hedley dialed 576-8900 and got a busy signal. "You hear that?" he said, holding the phone out to Janet Roscoe. "The line's busy."

"A minor inconvenience." Janet smiled. "One that your Mr. Winter must have foreseen."

"Right." Hedley replaced the receiver.

"So what's the drill?" she asked patiently.

"I wait five minutes and then try again."

"And if the line should be out of order?"

"I call the standby number, PLaza 3-2607. The same rule

applies to the primary number if I get the busy signal three times in a row."

"You have just the two numbers, the primary and the stand-by?" Kaplin raised a quizzical eyebrow. "That seems pretty inefficient to me."

"We didn't expect an emergency to arise this soon. Miles was supposed to find an alternative, but obviously he was otherwise occupied."

"With the so-called gate-crashers?" Kaplin sneered.

That was true of yesterday, but not Thursday. On Thursday, Miles would have taken steps to safeguard the letters in case anything did go wrong. Once he'd done that, it seemed likely that he'd spent the rest of the day trying to run Emsden to ground.

"Don't kid yourself, Kaplin," he said quietly. "They exist, they're not make-believe."

"So you keep telling us. But where's the proof?"

"What do you want? Abbott's body on the doorstep?" Hedley checked the time by his wristwatch and lifting the receiver, dialed the Madison Avenue number again. This time it rang out and went on ringing for a good two minutes before a breathless voice answered it.

"Who's that?" Hedley asked.

"It's me—Quirk."

"What kept you?"

"Oh, very funny," Quirk said tersely. "Now suppose you put Kaplin on the line. I might get some sense out of him."

Hedley relinquished the phone. From Quirk's angry response and the grim expression that subsequently appeared on Kaplin's face, he knew both men were convinced that he'd double-crossed them. Glancing in Janet's direction, he got the impression that she didn't share their opinion.

"That standby number of yours." Kaplin held the mouthpiece against his chest and snapped his fingers at Hedley. "Where's the pay phone located?"

"It's in Gluckstein's drugstore on East Forty-ninth Street.

I don't know the exact address, but it's somewhere between Fifth Avenue and Lexington Avenue."

Kaplin repeated the directions to Quirk and then slammed the phone down. "Did you get the drift, Hedley?" he said angrily. "Or do I have to spell it out to you?"

"You want me to call PLaza 3-2607."

Kaplin nodded curtly. "In twenty minutes from now," he added.

"We're wasting valuable time. Miles has been lifted and we should be looking for him."

"I don't want to seem defeatist," said Janet, "but that's easier said than done. We'd have had something to go on if he'd left a forwarding address with the Taft Hotel, but the way things are, I wouldn't know where to begin."

Hedley mulled it over. There was an outside chance that he could give them a starting point, but if he did so, it would mean disclosing yet another piece of information they could use against the SIS. The choice was simple enough, though: he either betrayed Abbott or Winter.

Deciding that Miles had to come first, he said, "Does the name Emsden mean anything to you?"

"No," said Janet. "Should it?"

"Emsden is a gossip columnist. We were going to use him to twist your arm. There's a faint possibility that he might be able to give us a lead. I know Miles tried to get in touch with him on Thursday, and it's conceivable he may have rung his office again last night after he'd spoken to me."

"Do you have Emsden's address?" Kaplin asked.

"He has an office in the J. C. Penney Building."

"And you think Abbott may have phoned him last night after 7:30?" Kaplin said scornfully. "Who do you suppose he spoke to—one of the security guards?"

"That's an assumption, Leo. I think we should check it out."

"You can't be serious, Jan."

"What have we got to lose?" Janet walked over to the writing desk and returned with the telephone directory. "What's Emsden's first name?"

"Walter," said Hedley. "He's also the features editor for *Rod and Gun* magazine."

"One thing at a time," she murmured as she ran a finger down the page. Then reaching for the telephone, she dialed 977-8711 and waited. "It's just an answering service," she said presently. " 'Please wait for the tone before leaving your message. In an emergency, I can be contacted at Seaview Cottage, Hyannisport, from Friday through Monday morning,' " she repeated. "I guess that last piece of information would convey something to Emsden's regular contacts."

"He'd need to be on the telephone," said Hedley. "Anyway, it's worth checking with directory inquiries or whatever you call it over here."

"He may not be listed. I have a feeling that where his personal life is concerned, Mr. Emsden would guard his privacy."

"I don't think we should give up that easily, Janet." Hedley glanced at her, wondering how she would react to the sudden and uninvited use of her Christian name, and saw a faint but amused smile.

"Who said anything about giving up?"

"Me, for one," said Kaplin. "As far as I'm concerned, this farce has gone on long enough. We should stop running around in circles and get our priorities straight."

Kaplin was a leg man and unlikely to go any higher, but he had a wealth of experience behind him and Hedley could see that his opinion carried a lot of weight with Janet. The furrowed brow and the way she explored her bottom lip with the tip of her tongue were two signs that told him he was losing out, but although he racked his brains for some convincing argument, his mind remained an obstinate blank.

"What time is it, Leo?" she asked quietly.

"Almost ten to eight. Quirk and Nolan should have reached the drugstore by now."

It was another way of saying they should try the standby number. Hedley lifted the receiver, dialed it, and got the same negative result—except that Quirk sounded even more aggrieved than he had on the previous occasion.

183

"I think you'd better talk to him," Hedley said, passing the phone to Kaplin. "He sounds ready to blow a gasket."

"He's not the only one."

Kaplin showed all the signs of a man with high blood pressure. His face was brick red and the veins stood out on his neck like cords. He was, Hedley thought, a candidate for a heart attack, a prognosis that would never apply to Janet Roscoe. Unlike Kaplin, who was almost incoherent with rage, she was cool and detached. The telephone directory had become a temporary writing pad resting on her thighs and she was busy jotting something down in a small notebook.

"Quirk's on his way back here," Kaplin said tersely and put the phone down.

"And Nolan?" she asked without looking up.

"I told him he could stand down."

"We'll need to get in touch with the police commissioner."

"Yeah? What for?"

"I want him to put out an APB on Abbott."

Kaplin stared at her, his mouth open. "An APB?" he repeated.

"There are two possible explanations for Abbott's sudden disappearance," she said calmly. "Either he has been snatched or else we've all been led up the garden path, and that includes Mr. James Hedley. Right from the outset we've concentrated on James, forgetting that Winter could be using him as sacrificial bait. By taking him, we've left the field wide open for Abbott."

"I hate to admit it," Hedley said slowly, "but you could be right."

He might have guessed that he had been set up. He had returned from Budapest expecting to be grilled for weeks on end, but instead the debriefing session with Deakin had lasted only a few hours. The question marks had been erased in one evening, and five days later Winter had sent him down to Portsmouth to look into the Crabb affair. At the time, he'd thought Winter was merely testing him, but now it looked as though it had simply been a ruse to create the impression that he'd been welcomed back into the fold.

"Well, the way I see it," said Janet, "finding Miles Abbott is the thing that really matters."

Hedley nodded. "You'll want his description?"

"I've already roughed something out. Listen to this and tell me what you think—Abbott, Miles: British subject, aged between thirty-four and thirty-six; height, 5'10"; weight, approximately 160 pounds; long narrow face with mole on left cheek and pale complexion; eyes, hazel; hair, light brown and parted on left side; when last seen, had a neat military-type mustache."

"You remember all that from the one car journey to Burnham House?" said Hedley.

"Have I got it right?"

"Well, I doubt if it makes any difference, but Miles was thirty-five."

"Why the past tense?" she asked quietly.

"Because I think he's dead," said Hedley.

Ladislav Bogach glanced at the speedometer and saw that the needle was hovering around eighty. Although Stamford, Bridgeport, and New Haven were behind him now, Hyannisport was still a good three hours hard driving away and he was tempted to keep his foot down. But a native caution warned him that while Interstate 95 might appear deserted, a police car could be lurking in a side road off the highway and he could well find himself in all kinds of trouble if they stopped him for speeding. For one thing, there was a 9mm Makarov automatic pistol complete with silencer in the glove compartment and for another, the license plates on the black Oldsmobile didn't match up with the vehicle registration. Easing his foot on the pedal, he allowed the needle to fall back to fifty.

He had called Abbott a liar when he'd told Panov and Zabrowski about Emsden, but he couldn't afford to back that hunch. Moscow had made it very clear that the British SIS operation had to be terminated at all costs, and he'd been around long enough to know what would happen to him if he failed. Bogach eyed the clock in the dashboard and tried to convince himself that another half hour on the journey was neither here nor there, but his stomach ulcer refused to believe it. The extra half hour meant that it would be past midnight before he arrived in Hyannisport, and it was essential he completed the return trip to New York before daybreak.

He could rely on Panov and Zabrowski to squeeze every last drop of information out of the Englishman before they killed him, but they still had to find Hedley and deal with him, and that was something they couldn't do on their own. Panov and Zabrowski were sleepers, agents who had lain dormant for ten years before he'd activated them, and it was necessary to supervise their every move.

For the second time in as many minutes Bogach glanced at the clock. He had six hours in which to find Seaview Cottage, deal with Emsden, and then drive 250 miles. Five, maybe ten years ago, he could have done it with ease, but now he wasn't so sure. *I'm getting old*, he thought, *and I've had enough*. Beria had sensed that back in '51. What had he said to him? "I've got just the job for you, Ladislav—chauffeur to our UNO delegate in New York. In theory you will be in charge of the NKVD detachment, but in practice you won't have to do much because all but the routine stuff will be handled by your deputy." Nothing could have been further from the truth; within two years the deputy had been recalled to Moscow and Beria had gone before a firing squad.

Bogach reared back, suddenly conscious that his eyelids were drooping. Old he might be, but he wasn't ready to die yet. Never one to believe in half measures, he wound the window down to let in the cold night air and then turned off the heater.

16.

Emsden was sprawled on the couch in front of the log fire, his shirt unbuttoned to the waist to expose a mat of dark, curly hair. He was nursing a glass of bourbon in his right hand and a Havana smoldered between the first and second fingers of his left. Already mellowed by a large T-bone steak washed down with a bottle of Nuit St. Georges, he realized the lissome blonde bumping and grinding to the beat of Frank Sinatra's *Songs for Swingin' Lovers* was beginning to make him feel decidedly horny. Her name was Stephanie Ifield; she was twenty-six years old and married to a congressman from Oregon who was, to use her words, a four-inch impotent jerk.

Emsden had met her ten days ago at a dreary cocktail party in Georgetown thrown by one of the White House aides. Washington was usually good for the odd salacious paragraph and, if nothing else, he'd hoped he might hear the latest on Eisenhower's cheese-paring household economies, but the aide, his wife, and the crummy guests they'd invited had been very straitlaced—with the notable exception of Stephanie Ifield. He'd come to the conclusion that the party was a dead loss and had been about to leave when he'd spotted her amongst a group at the far end of the drawing room.

She was wearing a dark green silk dress that fitted like a

sheath in all the right places and didn't leave much to the imagination. *Thirty-six, twenty-four, thirty-six,* he'd thought, sizing her up with a practiced eye, and then, as if suddenly conscious that he was staring at her, she had turned her head in his direction and smiled. There were all kinds of smiles—hesitant, shy, mocking, warm, enigmatic, icy, and loving—but the one Stephanie gave him was downright inviting. In the course of a few minutes conversation, she'd told him that her husband had just left Washington for Portland where he was campaigning for reelection, and he'd asked her for her telephone number. The following day, after lunching together at the Madison, they had driven off into the countryside and consummated their blossoming friendship in a motel ten miles south of Frederick.

It had been one of the most frantic and exhausting afternoons he'd experienced in a long, long time. "I needed that," Stephanie had told him after the first bout, and had rolled out of bed, padded across the room, and switched on the TV set. He had lain there wondering why the hell she wanted to see Eisenhower shaking hands with the voters in Portland and then suddenly she had pointed to a roly-poly figure trailing along in the rear of the president and squealed, "Now perhaps you can understand why—that's him—my husband—the four-inch jerk." There was no way he could tell whether the first part of her description was correct but he could see for himself that Ifield was a real asshole. With a perfect sense of timing, he'd nestled in close to Eisenhower and beamed into the camera, a round-faced buffoon, all teeth and glasses.

The newscast had confirmed Emsden's opinion that he was on to a good thing and fixing this weekend in Hyannisport had been a cinch. He had a few days between assignments, Ifield was still campaigning in Portland, and Stephanie had let it be known that her husband wasn't expecting her to join him out there until the final stretch, starting on Monday the twenty-ninth. Stephanie had flown into Boston that afternoon and, having picked her up from the airport, he'd made sure they arrived at Seaview Cottage well after dark. Tomorrow night he

188

would put her on a plane to Washington and no one, least of all the local residents, would be any the wiser. It was, he thought, a very discreet arrangement, but he was not short of practice at that kind of thing.

Emsden tossed his cigar into the log fire, swallowed the rest of the bourbon, and put the glass down on the floor. Crooking a finger, he beckoned to Stephanie. "Come on over here," he said.

"What for?"

"Give you one guess."

She came toward him, still swaying in time to the music, the skirt of her gray wool dress twirling high enough to give him an occasional glimpse of her knees. "This close enough?" she asked, staying just out of his reach.

"What do you think?"

"I think you've got that certain look in your eye."

"That makes two of us," he said.

She laughed and jived a little closer. Then, pretending to stumble over his outstretched legs, she fell on top of him. Her wet, open mouth fastened on his and her tongue went to work, slithering and coiling like a snake. A sex machine, he thought, and moved both hands under her skirt, raising it to caress the backs of her thighs. He wandered beyond the nylon hose, toyed briefly with a garter and groping higher still, began to fondle her butt.

"That's nice," she murmured, "but this is better."

"What is?"

"This," she said, and felt his erection. "You want to know the difference between you and Gerry?"

"I'm listening."

"With you, I don't end up with an aching wrist, that's the difference."

It was the kind of remark Emsden had come to expect of her, and he'd met few women lewder than Stephanie when she was aroused. Her deft fingers began to undo the buttons and sliding down, she knelt between his legs. Frank Sinatra finished on a soulful note, the record player cut out, and then the telephone started jangling.

"Aw, Jesus," he said. "Wouldn't you just know it."

"Let it ring," she whispered.

He wanted to follow her advice, but it was easier said than done. The phone went on repeating its strident summons and he found it impossible to sit back and enjoy what Stephanie was doing to him when the constant racket jarred his senses.

"It's no good," he grunted. "I've got to answer the god-damned thing." Emsden moved his hands, placed them on her shoulders and gently pushing her away, struggled to his feet and made it to the telephone. Snatching the receiver off the cradle, he spat out the Hyannisport number.

"Mr. Emsden?"

"That's me," he said. "Who are you?"

"My name is Janet Roscoe. I'm with the British Consular Office in New York."

Secretarial branch, he thought, *and locally employed.* A cool, well-educated young lady obviously dedicated to her job. Even so, no one in the Diplomatic would be working at this hour on a Saturday night unless there was a crisis of some kind, and that made her doubly interesting.

"Well now, Miss Roscoe," he said, turning on the charm, "what can I do for you?"

Stephanie made a face at him, pushed herself up from the floor, and walked over to the bar. Pouring a large measure of Scotch into a cut-glass tumbler, she removed the lid from the ice bucket and used a long-handled spoon to get at the cubes inside. Intent on showing her displeasure, she went out of her way to make as much noise as possible.

Turning his back on her, Emsden said, "I'm sorry, Mis Roscoe, but I'm having trouble hearing you. Would you mind repeating that?"

"I'm trying to locate a Mr. Miles Abbott."

"Yes?"

"I've reason to believe that he called at your office on Thursday."

Miles Abbott—the name sounded vaguely familiar but he

couldn't place it. "I was away in Chicago," he said. "As a matter of fact, I only spent a few hours in New York when I returned yesterday."

"Perhaps he left a message with your secretary?"

Emsden snapped his fingers. He had phoned the office from the airport to see if there were any messages for him and now that he came to think of it, his secretary had mentioned that some Britisher was anxious to get in touch with him.

"This Abbott," he said, playing for time, "would he be from England?"

"He did call at your office, then?"

Janet Roscoe was sharp, a little too sharp for his liking. Although tempted to deny it, Emsden thought it likely that she had already contacted his secretary.

"You're absolutely right," he said, "but I'm afraid he didn't leave a message. He asked for my address and told my secretary he'd get in touch with me later. Up to now I haven't heard another word from him."

"I see."

"Can you tell me why you want to trace him, Miss Roscoe?"

"It's to do with his family in England. I can't really say more than that."

Crap, Emsden thought, *pure crap*. Abbott had intimated that he had a juicy political story for him which would make the Teapot Dome scandal of 1923 seem very small beer by comparison. The allusion hadn't conveyed an awful lot to him: something about government officials and payoffs over a government-owned oilfield, he remembered. At the time, he'd figured Abbott had to be some kind of nut, but now he wasn't so sure. Now it was beginning to look as though there had been a story, one that the British were anxious to suppress for some reason.

"Well, obviously it's a personal and very urgent matter, otherwise you wouldn't have phoned me." Emsden sucked on his teeth. "Tell you what—I'll call the British Consular Office if I should hear from him again."

"That would be most helpful."

"You're welcome." Emsden slowly replaced the phone and

turned to face Stephanie.

"What was all that about, Walter?" she asked.

"Your guess is as good as mine." Emsden frowned. "I just don't understand how she knew that this guy, Abbott, had tried to see me."

"Your secretary could have told her."

"Maybe. But how and why did this Janet Roscoe get on to her in the first place?"

"Search me." Stephanie finished the Scotch and set the empty glass down on the bar. "Is it important?"

"You'd have to ask Janet Roscoe that, and she's not a very communicative lady."

"Really? I thought you two were getting along just fine."

"Not as well as we do," Emsden said and placed a hand on her thigh.

There was, Abbott decided, no avoiding the inescapable conclusion that Winter should have known better than to send him into the field. The pointers were all there buried in his personal file, and if Winter had taken the trouble to read between the lines, he would have realized that he'd always been a failure. If his long-suffering father hadn't sent him to a special tutor, he would never have passed the entrance examination to Sandhurst, and but for the war, he would have been thrown out on his ear after the first term. The elderly major commanding the depot at Bedford had quickly recognized his deficiencies as an infantry officer and had kept him at home training recruits while the first battalion was holding the perimeter at Dunkirk. The same thing had happened with SOE. True, he had broken both legs in a parachute jump, but the people at the top had seized the opportunity to post him to the Special Training School at Arisaig at a time when French-speaking agents were in short supply. Looking at it dispassionately, he supposed MI6 had only accepted him because somebody had to do the routine paperwork and he was known to be hard-working, loyal, reliable, and an efficient administrator.

Loyal and reliable: Abbott had lost count of the number of

times that assessment had appeared in his annual confidential report. The constant repetition had even convinced him that it was true, a correct evaluation of his character, but now he knew it was merely a stock phrase which various reporting officers had used to fill out a sentence whenever they couldn't think of anything else to say about him. Zabrowski and Panov had proved there was no truth in the appraisal; they had put his loyalty to the test and it had been found wanting. That was the stark, naked truth, even though it was a bitter pill to swallow

"Are you deaf, Miles?"

Abbott recognized Zabrowski's menacing voice and quickly raised his head, eyes blinking in the glare from the flashlight. "I can't hear you very well," he croaked.

"Some of the water must have run into his ears," said Panov.

"It's possible." Zabrowski drew on his cigarette, then dropped the stub onto the floor and crushed it under his heel. "Open your mouth, then close it and swallow hard, Miles."

"I already have," Abbott said thickly. "My ears just popped."

"Good. Now let's see if I've got this straight. You're now saying that you didn't send a letter to Emsden's Hyannisport address?"

"That's right."

"So why did you lie to us?"

"I was stalling." He tried to recall how much he'd already told them about Hedley, but in his exhausted state the memory cells refused to function. Listlessly deciding that Hedley would just have to look out for himself, he cleared his throat and went on, "I wanted to give Hedley time to clear out of the Algonquin and cover his tracks. I knew that would be the first thing he'd do when I didn't answer the 7:30 call."

"How very noble of you," Zabrowski said acidly.

"I also thought there was a chance you'd back off if I managed to convince you that Emsden already had some of the material."

"And if we didn't back off, Hedley would still have the means to go it alone?"

"Yes."

"Because you set up this post office box number for him in Seaford?"

"Yes. How many more times do I have to tell you?"

"Until we're sure we've got the whole truth," said Panov.

The water treatment had failed so they had resorted to caning the soles of his feet until they were swollen and covered with bloody bruises. He had stood it for as long as he could, but in the end they had broken him. Even if he had the will to do so, he was quite incapable of holding anything back, but it seemed Panov wouldn't be satisfied until he'd reduced him to a mindless vegetable.

Zabrowski said, "I think we're getting at the truth now, aren't we, Miles?"

"I've told you about the box number. What more do you want?"

"I just want to be certain I've got all the facts. You said it was 2075. Right?"

"Fuck you," Abbott said wearily. "I'm tired of your tricks. You know damn well it's 2077."

"If I got it wrong the first time, it's your fault for mumbling the way you do."

"Have you got any other complaints?"

"I'll let you know." Zabrowski lit another cigarette and inhaled deeply. "Tell us about the house, Miles—the one you rented on Division Avenue."

"It's about three miles out of town—a summer place—mostly timber except for the brick chimney. The nearest house is about seventy yards away but it's hidden from view by a belt of trees. It seemed to me that Two Acres was the kind of secluded place a writer might choose. That's why I decided to take it."

"A writer? Is that what Hedley is supposed to be?"

"Yes. I told the real estate people he'd pick up the key from them early next week." It was a lie, a final desperate attempt to salvage something. The key was waiting for Hedley at the post office in Seaford along with an invoice from Rai Sahib Hakison Lall.

"But Hedley won't go near the real estate office or the house, will he?"

"Why should he? He knows I only rented Two Acres to satisfy the post office." He had planted a seed of doubt; it showed in the way they looked at one another, and he knew they would cover both the house and the post office to be on the safe side.

"That makes sense to me," said Panov.

"Me too." Zabrowski trained the flashlight onto the bucket of water. "In fact, I'd say that about wraps it up."

There would be, Abbott thought dully, no prizes for guessing what would happen next. Right from the moment they'd disclosed their names to him, he'd known there was only one way the interrogation could end. They had believed him, that was the important thing, and for the first time in his life he hadn't been a total failure. They didn't know about the trinket box or the invoice, and in persuading them to cast a wider net around Seaford, he had reduced the odds against Hedley.

The chair went over backward and his head struck the floor again. Slowly, as if savoring every moment, Panov draped the towel over his face and then dipped the ladle into the bucket.

A mile and a half beyond Hyannisport, Bogach spotted the directional sign he was looking for in the grass border and braking hard, he turned off Chatham Road into the narrow dirt lane leading to Scaview Cottage. He thought there was a touch of poetic license about the name because the track went inland and it was doubtful whether Emsden had even a peep view of the ocean when the cottage was situated in a small hollow 100 yards from the main road. Shifting into neutral, he switched off the engine and, dousing the headlights, coasted silently up to the front porch.

There were no lights showing anywhere in the house, but he noticed the curtains were drawn in one of the front rooms and a Pontiac convertible was parked around the side under the carport. Leaning across the seat, he opened the glove compartment and took out the 9mm Makarov automatic. The box magazine was already loaded with eight rounds, but never one to leave anything to chance, Bogach removed it from the pistol grip and examined it under the courtesy light in the glove compartment to satisfy himself that the cartridges were seated properly. That done, he replaced the magazine, pulled the slide back to chamber a round, and pushed the catch up to safe. Twisting the silencer to make sure it was firmly locked into the grooves, he then tucked the automatic into the right-hand pocket of his overcoat and got out of the Oldsmobile.

The moon was partially obscured by dark scudding clouds and as he walked up the front steps, Bogach thought he could hear the surf breaking on the distant shore, but equally it could have been the wind rustling the fir trees. Jabbing the button in the illuminated panel on the door frame, he rang the bell and waited. A minute passed, then two, and getting no reaction, he pressed it again and held it down until a light came on in the hall.

A gruff voice said, "Who's there?"

"There's no need to be alarmed, Mr. Emsden," he said cheerfully. "My name's Daniel Bogach. I'm from the Boston office of the FBI. If you open the door a fraction, I'll show you my ID."

"You bet your sweet life you will." Emsden drew the bolts top and bottom, unlatched the door, and opened it as far as the security chain would allow. "Okay," he said, "let's see it."

"Certainly." Bogach produced a laminated card from the inside pocket of his topcoat and held it out for Emsden's inspection. "I'm sorry to disturb you at this hour, but it is important."

"Yeah?"

"You see, our people in New York arrested an Englishman called Miles Abbott a few hours ago and your name was mentioned in the preliminary interrogation."

"My name?" Emsden repeated. "Look, I know this Abbott called at my office in the J. C. Penney Building on Thursday morning but I never met the guy."

"I never said you did." Bogach slipped the fake ID into his pocket. "However, there are one or two routine questions I'd

196

like to ask you." He smiled fleetingly. "It shouldn't take more than a few minutes."

"You'd better come inside." Emsden removed the security chain, opened the door, and stepped aside to make room for Bogach. "What has Abbott been charged with?" he asked.

"Espionage," said Bogach.

"Is he a Commie?"

"We think so. Of course, he strongly denies it, but I've yet to meet a Communist agent who didn't."

"So McCarthy discovered. I covered most of the hearings of his Senate subcommittee and just about every other witness pleaded the Fifth Amendment."

Bogach followed Emsden into the lounge. A few embers from a log fire were still glowing in the heap of gray ash in the grate and a number of cushions were scattered about the floor. There was a pile of records on a chair and he spotted a couple of empty glasses amongst the disorderly array of bottles on the bar counter. Although it was hard to tell from where he was standing, it looked as if one of the tumblers was smeared with lipstick.

"Sit down. Make yourself comfortable." Emsden waved him to a chair. "Can I get you a drink?"

"No thanks, I've got a long drive in front of me."

"A tomato juice wouldn't hurt you."

"It's kind of you to offer but I'm not thirsty."

"Well, I sure am." Emsden walked over to the bar and opening a can of beer, poured it into a clean glass. "Something rather odd happened earlier this evening," he said casually. "A woman calling herself Janet Roscoe phoned me, inquiring after Abbott. She said she was with the British Consular Office in New York."

"What sort of accent did she have?"

"American. She had a pleasant voice, sounded well-educated."

"That could be his accomplice in the State Department," said Bogach. "You can bet she was using an alias."

"Yeah, that figures." Emsden perched himself on one of the

197

bar stools. "All the same, I don't understand why those two should want to get in touch with me."

"Some strips of microfilm were found inside the heel of Abbott's shoe. Pieced together, they give a very clear picture of our current thinking on the Suez Canal problem and the sanctions we could impose on the British and the French should they invade Egypt."

The fictional story sounded authentic and was sufficiently explosive to satisfy Emsden why it had been necessary for an FBI agent to call on him in the middle of the night. It was also the kind of news item that was bound to interest him, and his reactions in the next few minutes would tell Bogach what sort of man he was up against.

"I can see there would be one hell of a stink if that got out," said Emsden.

His voice was neutral but Bogach thought the way his eyes narrowed was significant. "Exactly," he said. "That's why Abbott sent you an extract. He posted it to this address on Friday."

"Really? Well, I haven't received it."

"The letter may turn up in your mail on Monday."

"If it does, I'll see you get it back unopened."

"Good." Bogach nodded emphatically. "I'm glad you appreciate this is a matter of national security." Emsden had been a shade too glib and while Abbott had almost certainly been lying when he'd told Zabrowski that he'd sent Emsden the registration slip from La Bouée Hotel, he couldn't afford to take any chances. "I'm sorry I had to drag you out of bed in the middle of the night," he said apologetically.

"Think nothing of it."

Bogach smiled and stood up. Withdrawing the Makarov automatic from the pocket of his overcoat, he thumbed the safety catch to fire and calmly squeezed off two shots. An incredulous expression appeared on Emsden's face, the glass slipped through his fingers and shattered on the floor and then, in slow motion, he toppled off the stool and went over backward, his head striking the bar as he fell down. The blood seeped through his dressing gown and within seconds his eyes were glazed and sightless. Turning away from him, Bogach went out into the hall to check the rest of the house.

The hall was L-shaped and a crack of light was showing under one of the doors in the corridor. As he moved toward the source of light, a sleepy disgruntled voice inside the room said, "Is that you, Walter?" Grunting in reply, Bogach opened the door.

The girl stirred and then suddenly, as if sensing that it wasn't Emsden who'd walked into the room, she sat bolt upright in the bed. Confused and frightened, she stared at him openmouthed and drew the bedclothes up to her chest to hide her naked breasts. Her mouth was still open, her throat still working to summon a scream when Bogach shot her in the head at point-blank range.

17.

Hemmed in by Greenpoint Avenue, the Expressway, Laurel Hill Boulevard, and Review Avenue, Calvary was the oldest and most crowded cemetery in Queens. Hedley thought it was also one of the most depressing places he'd seen in a long while. Against a backdrop of factory chimneys and the United Nations complex across the East River, acre upon acre of headstones, monuments, mausoleums, and obelisks stood shoulder to shoulder in huge plots separated by asphalt paths lined with gaunt, spindly trees.

As they turned off the main avenue and walked down one of the pathways toward the waiting ambulance, Nolan left the group of Homicide detectives clustered near a black, marble vault and came to meet them. Halting a few yards short of Janet Roscoe and Leo Kaplin, he removed the cigarette that was stuck to his lower lip and tossed the stub into a trash bin full of dead flowers.

"You were quick," he said. "I didn't expect you this soon."

"There wasn't much traffic on the roads," said Janet.

"Yeah, I forgot it was Sunday." Nolan scuffed a heel on the asphalt. "You want to look at the body?" he said, looking past Janet to Hedley.

"That's why I'm here, isn't it?"

"I guess it is. The rest of you had better stay here," Nolan said, waving a hand at Janet Roscoe, Kaplin, and Quirk. "Hedley's the only one who can identify the body."

"That's not strictly true," Janet said quietly. "Both Leo and I knew Miles Abbott by sight."

"We only need one witness," Nolan said firmly. Beckoning to Hedley, he turned about and walked off.

The body was lying ten yards in from the path on a strip of grass between the marble vault and a weather-beaten statue of a madonna and child. The head and trunk were covered by a black rubber sheet. Nolan bent down and flipped it aside.

"Is this Miles Abbott?" he asked in a flat voice. "Just answer yes or no."

"Yes." Hedley nodded. "Yes, it's Miles all right. What have they done to his mouth?"

"They sewed his lips together." Nolan replaced the sheet and stood up. "It's an old Mafia custom."

"They didn't kill him."

"I didn't say they did." Nolan took hold of his elbow and steered him toward the footpath where Janet Roscoe and the others were waiting. "No sense hanging about here," he said. "We'll only get in everyone's way."

Hedley glanced over his shoulder. Two ambulance attendants dressed in white overalls were busy zipping Miles into a waterproof bag before lifting him onto a stretcher, but the rest of the party around the vault had already started to break up, the medical examiner and the detectives from Homicide wandering off in separate directions.

"Where are they taking Miles?" he asked. "To a funeral parlor?"

"Not immediately," Nolan said tersely. "Homicide wants a postmortem done on him to establish the cause of death."

"Didn't they learn anything from the preliminary examination?"

The question went unanswered. Instead, Nolan glanced at Janet Roscoe and fished a notebook out of his raincoat pocket. "We have a positive ID," he said in a quiet voice.

Janet shook her head. "I'm sorry, James," she murmured, "really sorry."

"I know."

"Are you going to tell us what's in your little notebook?" Quirk unwrapped a stick of gum and popped it into his mouth. "Some of us would like to know the score."

"That figures." Nolan opened his notebook and turned over several pages. "The body was found at approximately 11:30 this morning by a Mrs. Elvira Innes, an elderly widow whose mother is buried in the plot opposite the madonna and child. The exact cause of death has yet to be established, but it's thought the deceased was drowned sometime between eight and midnight yesterday. Deep welts on the ankles, wrists, and upper arms indicate that the deceased had been bound hand and foot with thin pieces of rope or picture cord. Prior to that, the deceased had been rendered unconscious by a violent blow on the back of the skull which caused some venous bleeding."

"His name was Miles Abbott," Hedley said angrily. "Try using it. I don't like the word 'deceased.'"

"I've been a policeman for twenty years," said Nolan. "I have to be impersonal, it's the only way I can get by."

He turned over another page and continued in the same vein. "A total of twenty-three oval-shaped burns were found on the chest and neck, each measuring approximately one-half-inch long by three-sixteenths wide. The little finger on the right hand was swollen to twice its normal size and there were obvious signs that the knuckle had been broken. Finally, the soles of both feet were badly bruised and covered with blood blisters."

"You left something out," said Hedley. "They also sewed his mouth up with catgut."

"That was done later, after he was dead." Nolan closed his notebook and put it away.

"Why?" Janet whispered. "Why would they do a thing like that?" The color had gone from her face and she looked white and shaken.

"It's a message," said Quirk. "They're telling us that his

lips have been sealed."

Kaplin nodded. "I'd go along with that. They wouldn't have dumped his body here unless they wanted us to find it."

"That's a brilliant deduction," Nolan said acidly. "Do you want me to pass it on to Homicide?"

"You know damn well we don't."

"Homicide will be looking for a motive and they'll want to question Hedley. That's something you should think about."

"Nolan's right, Jan." Kaplin placed a hand under her elbow and gently shepherded her toward the main avenue where they had left the Cadillac. "We've got to put our heads together and come up with a plausible story."

"That's no problem," said Quirk. "We've already got Hedley lined up for possession of narcotics, so why don't we tie Abbott in with him? With $250,000 worth of uncut heroin at our disposal, it shouldn't be too difficult to plant the idea that Abbott had tried to double-cross the Mafia. How does that strike you, Jan?"

"I think it stinks," she said fiercely.

"So do I," said Hedley. "But it seems to me that you'll have to use Quirk's idea, at least in a modified form. Just about everybody in the N.Y.P.D. knows we put out an APB for Miles, and too many people were present when I identified his body. We need a logical explanation to satisfy their curiosity and linking Miles Abbott to that consignment of heroin is the only one we've got. You should find it simple enough to manufacture the evidence, but you'll have to give me time to fix a legend with Winter."

"What kind of legend?" Kaplin asked suspiciously.

They were only a few yards from the avenue now and Hedley could tell Nolan was growing more and more impatient. It showed in the way he kept snapping his fingers as if to remind them that time was running on and they weren't getting anywhere.

"Well, I think I'll have to become an undercover agent for C1. That's a branch of New Scotland Yard which deals with serious crimes affecting government departments. It's also responsible for the extradition of fugitive offenders."

"That sounds a plausible cover to me." Kaplin stopped by the Cadillac and leaned against the front nearside door. "What do you say, Jan?"

"It would certainly give James a good reason for being over here. Of course, we'd have to square it with the police commissioner, but I don't see any problem there."

"That's the story then, is it?" Nolan demanded impatiently. "Hedley is an English cop who came to New York armed with a warrant to extradite Abbott?"

"You've got it," said Kaplin.

"And if Homicide wants to question Hedley, they'll have to get in touch with the commissioner's office?"

"Yes."

"They're going to love that." Nolan turned about and walked away.

"There goes a happy man," Janet said dryly.

"You can say that again." Kaplin opened the car door for her. "This phone call to Winter," he said. "I suggest Hedley puts it through from our office downtown."

"I've got news for you," said Hedley. "Either I telephone him from the British Consulate on Third Avenue or we forget the whole thing."

"You've got a nerve."

"No, I'm just being practical, Kaplin. As soon as we've finished talking, Winter will have the call traced. If he suspects there were eavesdroppers on the line, he won't lift a finger, and then we'll all end up in the shit."

"James has a point, Leo."

"Don't listen to him, Jan. Every instinct tells me he's aiming to pull the rug out from under our feet."

Hedley said, "What if Miss Roscoe were to listen in on our conversation? Would that satisfy you?"

Kaplin thought it over, his lips pursed like a trumpet player. Finally, he passed the buck and said, "It's up to you, Jan."

"I say we do it his way, Leo. Now let's get out of here."

Kaplin closed the door after her and walked around to the other side. As soon as his back was turned, Quirk moved forward and planted himself in front of Hedley. "Do you mind telling me what gives between you and Jan?" he asked softly.

"What are you talking about?"

"Aw, come on, Hedley, you've got her eating out of your hand."

"You couldn't be more wrong."

"Yeah? It seems to me she's got the hots for you, old buddy." Quirk continued to move his jaws like a cow chewing the cud. "Maybe you two got together in London on the quiet." He nodded, a faint smile forming on his full lips. "Let me into a secret: How did you manage to persuade Jan to open her legs?"

Hedley looked in Kaplin's direction, saw that he was half in, half out of the Cadillac, and hit Quirk under the heart. The punch traveled less than six inches, but there was 180 pounds behind it and a lot of anger. The short arm jab took the wind out of Quirk and, swallowing the wad of chewing gum, he started to choke and buckled at the knees. Catching Quirk under the arms before he hit the ground, Hedley held the American upright and patted him on the back.

Kaplin said, "What the hell's going on?"

"Nothing," said Hedley. "Quirk's chewing gum just went down the wrong way, that's all."

The British Consulate in New York was staffed by one Consul General, two Deputy Consul Generals, four Consuls, and four Vice Consuls but, it being Sunday, the resident clerk was the only official on duty at 845 Third Avenue. After a somewhat heated discussion, the resident clerk agreed to telephone the duty Vice Consul, a process that continued progressively on up the chain as far as the second Deputy Consul General before Hedley got what he wanted and was allocated an office.

His problems, however, were only just beginning. There was a one-hour delay on the transatlantic switchboard and when the call finally did go through, he had to cope with a back echo on the line. Winter was not exactly overjoyed to hear from him either.

Hedley said, "We can close the investigation on Miles Abbott; he's had a fatal accident."

"When did this happen?" The response was low-key and calm, something Hedley had come to expect from Winter.

"Last night," Hedley said. "Sometime between eight and midnight. The police doctor thinks he was drowned, but we won't know that for sure until after the autopsy. I imagine there will be an inquest."

"I see."

Winter was still playing the waiting game, giving him no help at all, and it wasn't difficult to guess what was uppermost in his mind. He had made it very clear that his private number was only to be used as a last resort and undoubtedly he was wondering just how he could extricate himself from the mess.

"I need some guidance." Hedley paused. The line was insecure and he would have to get the message across in veiled speech, which wasn't going to be easy. "For instance, what do I tell the coroner?"

"Whatever is necessary. I presume you've made your number with the N.Y.P.D.?"

The fencing had stopped. Winter had seen the light and had given him the opening he needed. "I met the commissioner on Friday and presented the extradition warrant for Abbott." He paused again, waited until the back echo had died away, and then said, "According to McNulty, the consignment of heroin arrived here the day before I did. Abbott sent it over in a diplomatic bag addressed to the British Information Service. The docket was marked To Await Collection."

"That was a cunning move," Winter said wryly.

"It certainly was. We were hoping Abbott would collect it eventually, but of course that's all gone by the board now. I don't know what's going to happen to the evidence."

"Have they impounded it?"

When it came to veiled speech, Hedley thought Winter had

few equals. "The situation is a little confused," he said guardedly.

"Try and get it back. We'll need the heroin as evidence when we charge Abbott's accomplice."

"I'll do my best but I'm going to need all the help I can get from C1 to pull it off." The message seemed clear enough to him but he decided to ram it home just in case there was any doubt in Winter's mind. "I'm afraid there's likely to be a clash of interests."

"So I've already gathered."

"One final point," said Hedley. "I'm phoning from the British Consulate and they're anxious to know what arrangements Abbott's next of kin would like them to make. Perhaps you could get in touch with them?"

The question hung in the air for what seemed an eternity as Winter thought it over. Finally, just when it seemed he was about to wash his hands of the whole affair, he said, "Leave it to me, Superintendent. I'll telephone his father tonight."

"Thank you," Hedley said and meant it.

"You don't have to," said Winter. "It's part of my job."

A faint clatter abruptly severed the connection and terminated their conversation on a sour note.

"How did you make out?" Janet asked quietly.

"I got what I wanted," Hedley said, and put the phone down.

"You could have fooled me. You looked so grim that I thought Winter had turned you down."

"No, I was just thinking about Miles and how little I really knew him. I saw him as Winter's errand boy, a man who was strong on theory but without practical experience. All Miles ever told me about himself could have been gleaned from his record of service. His personal life was, and still is, a closed book to me."

"Maybe that's how it should be."

Perhaps he was twisting her words, but it sounded like a discreet hint that they should bury the whole mess along with Miles. "I'll make a deal with you," he said slowly. "I'll give you the letters in return for the men who killed Miles."

"It wouldn't be an equitable arrangement," she said. "I doubt if I could deliver my side of the bargain."

"You're wrong, Janet." Hedley stretched out a hand and touched her shoulder. "I know when and where we can nail them."

He could see that she was interested, and he told her about his last conversation with Miles and the significance of the post office box number and just why he believed the opposition would be waiting for him in Seaford on Monday morning.

Winter crumpled the sheet of crested writing paper into a ball and tossed it into the wastepaper basket. He had already telephoned the general to inform him that Miles was dead and after six previous attempts, he now knew that this urge to write a letter of condolence was simply a desire to exorcise a nagging feeling of guilt. Lieutenant General Sir Hugh Abbott, KCB, DSO, MC would have understood the subtle hints and pressures that had prompted him to set up the operation, but it was despicable to shed part of the burden on to the shoulders of a lonely old man merely to ease his conscience. His first duty was to clear up the mess he'd created.

Providing Hedley with the cover he wanted was not going to be easy but with his contacts at Scotland Yard, Cleaver would be able to pull a few strings and in all the years they'd known each other, Malcolm had yet to let him down. Much of the spadework had already been done by Hedley because from what he'd said on the telephone, it was quite evident that he'd made a deal with McNulty's associates in New York and they were obviously prepared to back his story. It was also very clear to him that they wouldn't have agreed to do that unless Hedley was in a position to deliver the Eisenhower letters to them.

He wondered what the CIA would do with the letters. Perhaps they figured they could use them to twist his arm but if so, they were mistaken. The axe would fall on his neck long before they could approach him, because the whole story would come out tomorrow when he arranged for Miles to be flown home at his expense. No doubt the Foreign Office would have kittens about it, but Bracecourt owed him the odd favor and the Americans were unlikely to place any obstacles in their way.

He wished he could dig a grave for Turnock while he was at it, but somebody else would have to do that and it would be a lengthy job. Turnock had achieved his aim and now that the operation was a busted flush, he was unlikely to see Rida again. There was, however, a distinct possibility that Korznikov might try to recruit him and once he knew the facts, Control would ensure that he was kept under surveillance. Special Branch would need to play it very carefully because he was damn sure that Turnock knew he was being watched. It was the only explanation that Winter could think of for his quite extraordinary about-face. Until a few days ago, Turnock had been bitterly opposed to the Suez invasion, but almost overnight he had become the most ardent of converts.

Winter pushed the chair back and stood up. Thinking about Turnock only made him angry and that didn't solve anything. Leaving the study, he crossed the hall and went into the drawing room. The television was still going full blast and he noticed that Geraldine had nearly finished the half-pound box of Cadbury's chocolates that was balanced on the arm of her chair.

"You were a long time," she said without taking her eyes off the screen.

Winter fixed himself a large whiskey and soda. "I had some bad news," he said quietly.

"Concerning Katherine?"

"No, it was about a fatal accident that has happened to one of my subordinates."

"Oh." Geraldine dipped into the box for another soft-centered chocolate and popped it into her mouth. "I feel so sorry for Harry," she said. "I mean, how is he going to cope with three children on his own?"

"You're being a little premature, aren't you? Katherine isn't dead yet."

"One has to face the facts, Charles. The tumor is malignant. Harry told us so."

She's guessed, he thought, *she's guessed that Katherine and I were lovers and this is her way of getting back at me.* Well, he wouldn't give Geraldine the satisfaction of knowing that the knife thrust had sunk in.

"What are you watching?" he asked, firmly changing the subject.

"Sunday Night at the Palladium."

Encouraged by Tommy Trinder, a young couple dressed in satin track suits were trying to cram as many balloons into a tea chest as they could. Their task appeared ludicrously simple at first sight, but the balloons were filled with helium and kept rising into the air.

"Beat the Clock," said Geraldine.

"What?"

"This game," she said. "It's called Beat the Clock."

Winter smiled. The name was not inappropriate. Tomorrow afternoon at four o'clock, Colonel Ariel Sharon's brigade would cross the frontier into Sinai at Suweilma and exactly an hour later, one of his parachute battalions would be dropped fifteen miles east of the Mitla Pass. According to Bracecourt, the Anglo-French ultimatum would be delivered sometime the following day, and that meant he had less than forty-eight hours to beat the clock and extricate Hedley before the balloon went up.

18.

The sky had been a melancholy gray when they left the house on West Fifty-sixth Street and the weather had taken a turn for the worse after they'd crossed the Williamsburg Bridge into Brooklyn, the persistent drizzle suddenly becoming a heavy downpour. Driving conditions were still bad when they'd joined Route 27 and, playing it safe, Janet Roscoe had switched on the headlights and stayed well under the speed limit. Then, just beyond Lynbrook, the sky cleared and the sun broke through the puffy cumulus clouds as if to herald a bright new morning.

"Perhaps it's a good omen," Janet suggested with a faint smile.

"Let's hope so." Hedley glanced into the rearview mirror, saw that the Plymouth sedan had closed in on them, narrowing the distance between the two vehicles to less than fifty feet, and immediately reached for the microphone under the dashboard. "Our friend Quirk is too damn close," he said tersely. "I'm going to tell him to drop back."

"He won't listen to you."

"All right, you talk to him."

Janet shook her head. "I'd be wasting my breath."

Hedley knew she was right, and he replaced the microphone.

Kaplin had given Quirk explicit instructions that he was to stick to them like a limpet until they reached the rendezvous two miles west of Seaford. "I don't trust you, Hedley," Kaplin had told him. "We've only got your word for it that this post office box number is in Seaford. For all we know, it could be someplace else."

"What does Kaplin think I'm going to do?" he said, voicing his thoughts aloud. "Grab the wheel, push you out of the car, and take off?"

"You ought to know by now that Leo doesn't leave anything to chance."

"Yes, that's his style, I guess." Hedley lit a cigarette and opened the ashtray in the dashboard. "I bet he's even got somebody watching Emsden's cottage up at Hyannisport."

"Actually, that was my idea." Janet flicked the indicator down to signal that she was leaving the highway and turning right at the interchange ahead. "And there's something else you should know. Emsden has been murdered. The duty officer at Zenith rang me at four o'clock this morning, shortly before Leo set off for Seaford. It seems Emsden was shacked up with a lady friend, a blonde in her mid-twenties. She had been shot through the head from close range."

It wasn't difficult to guess the motive for the double murder. The opposition had stretched Miles to the limit of his endurance and he'd turned the spotlight on Emsden, perhaps hoping it would buy him a little time. No one would ever know what had passed through his mind, but Hedley guessed that Miles had figured there was a chance his interrogators would back off if he managed to convince them that Emsden already had some of the blackmail material.

"Do you have any idea when they were killed?" he asked presently.

"It must have been sometime late on Saturday night, but your guess is as good as mine." Janet shrugged her shoulders. "Our people didn't hang about long enough to find out. However, they did say that the killer had certainly gone out of his way to make it look as though the cottage had been burglarized.

Every room was in a shambles, the furniture overturned, the contents of the closets and chests of drawers scattered all over the floor."

"A burglary that ended in a double murder?" said Hedley. "Is that how the local police see it?"

"They don't know about Emsden and the girl yet. We thought it best to keep the information to ourselves. It saves answering a lot of awkward questions."

Hedley thought it was also the only way they could avoid a lot of unfavorable publicity. Stubbing his cigarette out in the dashboard ashtray, he picked up the road map lying on the bench seat between them. They were heading east on a minor road that ran parallel with Route 27 and he recalled that a few miles back they'd passed the entrance to Milburn Creek.

"Hadn't you better slow down?" he said. "We must be getting near the rendezvous."

"It's still about two miles ahead," Janet said confidently, and then, contrarywise, eased her foot on the pedal until the speedometer was showing thirty miles an hour.

Kaplin viewed the forest clearing with a jaundiced eye. They had picked it off the map, thinking it would make an ideal rendezvous but now, having seen the place at first hand, he wasn't entirely sold on it. The trees were almost bare and there were no convenient bushes where a vehicle could be hidden away. The ground was also carpeted with fallen leaves and soft underfoot, which meant watching where you were driving if you didn't want to end up axle deep in mud. However, the glade was a good mile from the Seaford Road and he could see from the empty litter baskets dotted around the picnic area that nobody else had been near the beauty spot in weeks.

Trudging across the clearing to the nearest picnic table, he sat down on the wooden bench and unfolded his map. Placing it facedown on the table, he took out a ballpoint and began to draw a sketchmap of Seaford, indicating the police station, the post office, and some of the bigger stores. Extending Main Street eastward, Kaplin showed Division Avenue joining it at right angles and then marked the approximate position of Two Acres. Immediately behind the house, a narrow open-ended oblong represented the creek due north of Goose Island. Satisfied with his handiwork, he unearthed a few pebbles and used them to weight the map at the corners.

Kaplin yawned and stretched both arms above his head. There was a time when he could have gone without sleep for several days on end and felt little the worse for it, but now it seemed old age was finally catching up on him. He decided a quick shave would freshen him up, and set off toward the green and white two-tone Chevrolet to collect his battery shaver. Halfway across the clearing he stopped in midstride and canted his head to listen intently. The noise was faint and a long way off. Thinking it could be a light aircraft, he looked up at the sky.

The noise grew steadily louder and the beat seemed uneven to his ears, as if the engines were not synchronized. Two vehicles, he thought, and coming this way. He turned half right to watch the entrance to the glade and moments later saw the chrome-and-mouth organ front of a Chrysler. As Janet braked to a halt a few yards in front of him, Quirk swept into the clearing and drew up alongside the Chrysler. Smiling, Kaplin moved forward to open the door for Janet.

"Hi," she said. "How's it going?"

"Pretty good. Everything's set up in town." Kaplin pointed to the picnic table. "I drew a sketchmap of Seaford while I was waiting. I figured it might give you a rough idea of what the town is like." Signaling Hedley and Quirk to follow them, Kaplin fell in step with Janet. "I've talked to the chief of police," he said in a low voice. "He was a mite curious to know what the CIA was up to in this neck of the woods, but I phoned headquarters at Langley and they soon straightened him out."

"And?" Janet prompted.

Kaplin smiled. "The chief suddenly became very cooperative. You and I will be working direct to him on a one-to-one radio link, just the way you wanted."

"Good." Janet glanced at the sketchmap on the table.

"You're quite an artist, Leo," she said.

"Thanks." Kaplin picked up a twig and indicated the horizontal line on the sketch. "This is Main Street," he said, looking straight at Hedley. "As you drive into town from here, the first thing you'll see is a Mobil filling station on your right. The next landmark of any consequence is a supermarket on the opposite side of the road and then, two blocks beyond it, you'll see the Plaza movie theater on the corner of Main and Union streets. The post office is directly opposite the movie theater, next door to a hardware store."

"I don't see any scale." Hedley tapped the map with his fore-finger. "How far is the post office from the Mobil filling station?"

"Six-tenths of a mile," said Kaplin. "I clocked it on the odometer."

"I see. What's the box in front of the post office?"

"That's supposed to be Independence Square."

The rest of the sketchmap was less detailed. There were a number of spines branching off from Main Street, but apart from showing Division Avenue and the approximate position of Two Acres, Kaplin hadn't bothered to name any of the side roads.

"All right," said Hedley. "How do you propose to cover me when I walk into the post office?"

"I'll be in the parking lot behind the supermarket and in radio contact with the chief of police." Kaplin pointed to a flashing beacon which he'd drawn in a side street one block from the filling station on the outskirts of Seaford. "Meanwhile, Jan will be inside the supermarket watching Main Street. She will have a pocket-size field radio so that we can keep in touch with one another. Quirk will follow you into town and then position himself on Division Avenue, facing north. You get the picture?"

Hedley nodded. The picture was a good deal clearer to him than Kaplin imagined. The opposition would be armed and he wouldn't, and while Janet could observe his every move, the supermarket was a good twenty-five yards from the post office.

A distance of that order gave the opposition a definite edge and he just hoped she would be quick off the mark if anything went wrong.

"I presume you'll want a head start on me?" he said.

"Ten minutes should be enough. Then you can move out." Kaplin reached inside his leather jacket and handed Hedley back his passport. "You'll need this to prove your identity."

A foreign government and its accredited agents and representatives were required to afford him protection. That was the gist of the flowery language inside the cover of his passport, but right now, Hedley wished he had the same kind of bulge under his jacket that Kaplin had, rather than a facsimile expressing the pious hopes of Her Majesty's Foreign Secretary.

Janet said, "I doubt if you need my advice, James, but park the Chrysler as near as you can to the post office and stay in the shadows when you get out."

"Don't you worry," said Hedley, "my right shoulder will be cleaning the plate glass window of the hardware store."

"Good—you do that." She smiled, wished him good luck and then, nodding to Kaplin, she turned and walked off toward the Chevrolet.

Two miles away in Seaford the post office was about to open for business.

Zabrowski pulled into the curb outside Watson and Bull's real estate office in Independence Square and switched off the ignition. Opening the offside cab door, he climbed out of the Ford pickup, walked around to the front, and raised the hood. For some moments he stood there frowning at the engine, then, muttering to himself, he returned to the cab and opened the tool bin. Still mumbling away, he moved the jack and tire levers aside and dug out a greasy canvas wallet.

The truck was seven years old and in a battered condition, but despite the raised hood there was nothing wrong with the engine. Approaching Seaford from the direction of West Amityville, Zabrowski had stopped a mile from the outskirts of town to loosen the low tension lead from the coil to the distributor.

It was an old dodge from way back: from then on the engine had sounded as if it were being starved of gas. On-street parking was allowed in Independence Square, but only for twenty minutes in any one hour and he'd wanted a cast-iron excuse for staying longer. Nor was it by chance that he'd broken down outside the real estate office. Bogach had spent the previous afternoon reconnoitering the town with him and they had chosen that particular site because it afforded a commanding view of the post office, which lay diagonally across the square from Watson and Bull.

The recce had also convinced them that Seaford was not the place to ambush Hedley; the town was too small and with only one route in and out the chances of making a successful getaway were next to zero. Faced with those constricting factors they had made two contingency plans. The first was based on a hunch that the letter waiting for Hedley at the box number might direct him to the house on Division Avenue where Bogach and Panov were now lying in wait. The second was founded on the premise that the information they'd received from Abbott was correct in that Hedley would drive straight back to New York after calling at the post office. If that should be the case, then it was their intention to bounce him somewhere on a deserted stretch of the road between Seaford and the state highway.

Zabrowski opened the canvas wallet, took out a small open-ended wrench, and began to undo the union joint which secured the copper feed pipe to the carburetor. Working slowly, he slackened the nut off, allowed a dribble of gasoline to escape, and then tightened the joint again. The post office had opened ten minutes ago but although there were a fair number of people about, nobody had gone near the place as yet.

Still going through the motions, Zabrowski unscrewed and removed the air cleaner and made a thorough inspection of the carburetor. A prowl car came down Main Street, moving slowly, and with baited breath, he watched it turn right into Union Street. Blowing a few particles of dust out of the filter, he replaced the air cleaner and tightened the wing nuts.

The minutes crawled by: five, ten, fifteen, and the sweat began to trickle down his nose. He couldn't think why Hedley hadn't shown up yet; in his shoes, he would have been outside the post office waiting for the doors to open. Maybe they'd underestimated Abbott? Maybe he'd deliberately sent them to the wrong town? No, that was impossible. By the time they had finished with him, Abbott had been only too eager to tell them everything they wanted to know.

Zabrowski put the open-ended wrench down and wiped both hands on his greasy overalls. Out of the corner of his eye, he saw a Chrysler pull into the curbside near the hardware store, and then a tall, dark-haired man got out of the sedan and walked toward the post office. Although the passport photograph which Bogach had received from London showed a more youthful-looking Hedley, there was no mistaking the rugged outlines of his face even from a distance of sixty feet. Leaning inside the cab, he called Bogach on the two-way radio to advise him that their target had arrived in town. That done, he swiftly tightened the low tension lead, dropped the hood, and packed his tools away. He was ready to follow Hedley the moment he walked out of the post office.

Hedley walked into the post office and found he had the place more or less to himself. Behind the counter, a small elderly woman was busy sorting the mail, pigeonholing the letters into the appropriate mailboxes that spanned the length of the far wall from the floor to a height of six feet.

"Morning," she said, her back still toward him. "I'll be with you in a minute."

"That's all right," said Hedley. "I'm in no hurry."

"You're not from these parts," she said.

"No, I'm from England."

"England," she murmured. The last letter disappeared into a box and she turned about, her eyes smiling behind gold-rimmed spectacles. "You're a long way from home."

"I'm a writer," he said, as if that explained everything.

"Oh my," she said, "a writer. We don't get to meet many

authors in Seaford. Are you staying here or just passing through?"

"A friend has rented me a house on Division Avenue."

"Two Acres?"

"That's right."

"Then you must be Mr. James Hedley."

"Right again."

"I remember your friend coming here on Friday. He's English too, isn't he?"

"Yes, he works for a literary agency on Third Avenue." Her eyes widened and he guessed the news would be all over town before the day was out.

"My," she breathed, "that must be a fascinating job."

"Yes, it is." Hedley smiled and pushed his passport under the grille. "Do you happen to know if there are any letters waiting for me? My box number is 2077."

"2077? Well now, let's see what we have." The postmistress moved to the other end of the counter and opened a box on the fourth row. "One from New York City," she said, reading the postmark, "posted AM Saturday."

The long shot had paid off. Sometime after their telephone conversation on Friday night, Miles had sat down and written him a letter. In all probability, he'd purchased the stamps when he'd rented the mailbox.

"Thank you."

"You're welcome." Her plump, round face beamed at him through the grille. "Have a nice day."

Hedley pocketed the letter and his passport, wished her the same, and walked out of the post office. Turning left outside, he strolled back to the Chrysler, opened the door, and got in.

So far so good, he thought, and fished the letter out of his pocket. Ripping open the envelope, he found it contained a sales invoice from Rai Sahib Hakison Lall's emporium on Thirty-fourth Street and a key wrapped inside a fancy paper napkin with Larré's French Restaurant printed across one corner. There were a few brief lines on the back of the invoice which read: "Enclosed is the front door key to Two Acres. I bought a large trinket box from Rai Sahib—typically Indian with lots of ornate carving and a false compartment in the bottom—no prizes for guessing what it contains! I hocked the box on Thursday afternoon. You'll find the pawn ticket in the bathroom—top shelf of the medicine cabinet."

Hedley stared at the invoice. Renting a deposit box would have been a simpler and more effective way of safeguarding the letters, but banks were notoriously slow and they would have asked Miles for several references, which of course he couldn't supply. He wondered if Miles had told the opposition about the box and what he'd done with it. If he had, they were on a wild-goose chase and somewhere in New York a pawnbroker was probably lying dead on the floor of his shop.

Reaching for the microphone under the dashboard, Hedley pressed the transmit button and said, "We're on a treasure hunt; the box number was just a signpost along the way. Our next stop is Two Acres."

Kaplin said, "Roger. Don't move from your present location until we close up. You read me?"

Hedley gave him a terse "willco" and then checked his wrist-watch. He calculated that it would take Janet no more than two minutes to leave the supermarket and scramble into the waiting Chevrolet. Kaplin would already have the motor running and seconds later they would pull out of the parking lot. Allowing them a little leeway, he figured their vehicle would appear in his rearview mirror at exactly 9:50.

Hedley switched on the ignition and cranked the engine into life. Still warm, the motor caught the first time and, taking his foot off the accelerator, he left it to tick over. From time to time he glanced into the mirror but for the most part he looked straight ahead, searching the buildings on the far side of Independence Square through eyes narrowed against the glare. There was a public library on the corner and from the flat roof a sniper would have a perfect field of fire. The sun was shining on the windshield of the Chrysler, but that was unlikely to put him off his aim. A marksman would center the crosswires a few inches above the steering column, knowing the high velocity bullet would strike him in the chest.

Nine-fifty came and went, and still there was no sign of the Chevrolet. A woman came out of the hardware store, got into the Buick station wagon which was parked in front of him, and drove off.

Feeling more exposed than ever, Hedley grabbed the mike and called Kaplin again. "What's the holdup?" he snapped.

"We have a slight mechanical problem," Kaplin said calmly. "The carburetor has flooded."

"That does it," said Hedley. "I'm not waiting here any longer like a sitting duck. Tell Quirk I'm on the way."

Kaplin was still in full voice when he slammed the gearshift into first and pulled away from the curb. With a triumphant smile on his face, Zabrowski watched the Chrysler drive past him on the other side of the square and then called Bogach on the two-way radio.

Bogach tossed the portable field radio on to the bed, drew a chair up to the open window, and sat down. The bedroom was above and slightly to the left of the porch, and Hedley would have to cross a wide expanse of lawn to reach the front door. He would never make it. Panov had taken cover in the large clump of rhododendrons which bordered the lawn on the right, and Hedley would be caught in their crossfire and cut down before he was halfway there. Two Acres enjoyed a secluded position: there were no houses across the avenue and the nearest property on either side was a good seventy yards away, one screened from view by a thick belt of trees, the other by a sharp bend in the road. It was a perfect site for an ambush; nobody would hear the shots because of the silencers and nobody would see Hedley fall.

Everything had gone like clockwork so far, and Bogach saw no reason why it shouldn't continue that way. They had moved into Division Avenue late on Sunday evening, driving silently and without lights so that none of the neighbors should see or hear them. Driving quietly past Two Acres, they had turned off the road onto a dirt track that led down to the creek. Parking the Oldsmobile amongst the sand dunes where it was out of sight, they had made their way back to the house and broken in through the French windows on the patio. A prowl car had visited the neighhorhood twice during the hours of darkness, its spotlight sweeping the darkened house, but apart from those few nerve-racking moments, the rest of the night had been uneventful.

Bogach glanced to his right and wondered how Panov was making out. Panov had moved into position shortly before dawn when it had been bitterly cold. No doubt his hip flask had kept him warm but he just hoped Panov hadn't drunk too much of the hard stuff because, any minute now, Hedley would come bowling down the avenue.

Although Kaplin had told him that Hedley was on the way, Quirk was still facing north, twenty feet from the T-junction, when the Chrysler turned into Division Avenue. Determined that Hedley wasn't going to make a monkey out of him, he wanted to be damn sure the son of a bitch really was heading toward Two Acres before he made a three-point turn.

Waving the Englishman to continue on down the avenue, Quirk shifted into first, swung diagonally across the road and locking the wheel hard over to the right, braked to a halt and selected reverse. In his eagerness to catch up with Hedley, he let the clutch out too fast and stalled the Plymouth ten feet out from the curb. By the time he restarted the engine and was ready to back up, Zabrowski was approaching the T-junction from the direction of Seaford.

Dropping into third, Zabrowski signaled that he was turning right. The speedometer was registering a shade over twenty when he swept into Division Avenue and saw a Plymouth diagonally across the road. The vehicle was stationary but before he could blast a warning, the driver started to move forward, cutting in front of him.

Zabrowski swerved to the right, mounted the sidewalk, and headed straight at one of the few streetlights on the avenue. He stamped on the footbrake, but somehow the outside edge of his shoe also pressed down on the accelerator and he hit the steel bollard at thirty miles an hour. The impact smashed the radiator into a neat V shape and sheered the engine from its mounting bolts, driving it back through the rear bulkhead. An invisible force plucked Zabrowski from the driving seat and sent him headfirst through the windshield. The shards of glass ripped his face to pieces and put out his left eye, but it was the steering column which disemboweled and killed him, penetrating four inches into his stomach above the navel and ripping downward as he sailed through the air to land on the hood.

Quirk hesitated, uncertain what to do. Then, deciding Hedley was his primary concern, he put his foot down and left the carnage behind him. At that precise moment in time, Kaplin and Janet Roscoe were some 200 yards from the scene of the accident.

Hedley pulled up outside Two Acres, opened the car door, and started to get out. One foot was on the sidewalk when he heard the crash, and he froze, half in, half out of the Chrysler. Then, shaking off the momentary torpor, he scrambled out of the sedan and ran back to see what had happened to Quirk.

Bogach too had heard the crash, and he swore. He'd taken aim and was waiting for Hedley to come nearer before squeezing the trigger, but now, instead of approaching the house, the Englishman had turned away from it, presenting him with a slim, fast-moving target. Tracking Hedley with the Makarov automatic, he realigned the foresight blade and, at a range of seventy feet, fired twice in rapid succession. The first round struck the rear fender with a loud clunk, the second hit the sidewalk a few inches in front of Hedley and ricocheted off.

Hedley saw the puff mark in front of him and dived into the gutter, both arms outstretched to break his fall. Landing heavily, he pressed himself flat, seeking what protection he could from the curbstone. The belt of trees which screened Two Acres from the neighboring property was some ten yards away and, wriggling like a snake, he wormed his way forward.

Quirk saw Hedley crawling toward him in the gutter and,

swerving out on to the crown of the road, he stomped on the brakes and slewed to an emergency halt. Throwing the door open, he snatched the Colt .357 Police Positive from his hip holster and tumbled out of the Plymouth. He hadn't the faintest idea what was going on, but common sense told him that Hedley wasn't crawling along on his belly for fun. It was also very clear to him that the belt of trees was the best cover around, and breaking into a run, he cut across the lawn straight into Panov's line of fire. Bent almost double, Quirk heard a loud crack as a bullet passed above his head, and skidding to a halt, he whirled half left and fired at the clump of rhododendrons.

Bogach hesitated momentarily, unsure which of the two men he should take first. Hedley, who was up and running for the belt of trees, was the primary target, but the man directly below him was armed and there were strong grounds for thinking the Englishman wasn't. Hesitating no longer, he took aim and fired. The bullet struck Quirk in the neck and boring down through his chest at an angle of forty-five degrees, it exited below the left rib cage. The impact swung him around so that for a millisecond he pirouetted on tiptoe like a ballet dancer, his arms outstretched as if to embrace the sky. As he toppled over, the Colt left his right hand and hit the ground ten feet beyond his lifeless body.

Kaplin turned into Division Avenue, saw the wrecked pickup, and immediately applied the brakes.

"Leave it, Leo," Janet shouted. "Put your foot down and keep going."

"I can't," he snapped. "The guy looks in a bad way."

Two housewives were already running toward the scene of the accident, but it was evident that Leo doubted if they would be of much help. Reaching for the mike, Janet contacted the chief of police in Seaford, reported their location, and asked for an ambulance. Then, turning to Kaplin, she told him to move on in no uncertain terms. One of the housewives shook her fist at them as they drove past but although Kaplin turned brick red, the angry gesture didn't ruffle Janet.

Hedley stared at the revolver lying on the lawn some twenty-five feet to his front. There were two gunmen: one in the bedroom above the front porch, the other somewhere in the clump of rhododendrons, and prudence counseled him to stay put until Kaplin showed up. Certainly that was the sensible thing to do, but he was tired of playing it safe. Breaking cover, Hedley raced forward, swerving left and right to present a difficult target. Eight yards seemed more like a hundred and, making a swallow dive, he grabbed the Colt with both hands, rolled over onto his left side, and fired up at the bedroom window.

A shot plowed into the lawn a few inches from his face and, flipping over onto his stomach, he saw a wisp of smoke rising from the rhododendrons. Elbows braced and using a double-handed grip to steady the Police Positive, he aimed slightly below the telltale discharge and squeezed the trigger.

A tall thin man staggered out of the bushes clutching his side, and taking aim again, Hedley shot him in the stomach before rolling over and over to reach the porch. For some reason, the gunman above had stopped firing, but he didn't stop to question why. Staying close to the wall, he straightened up and began to edge his way toward the back door. As he rounded the corner and started running, Kaplin pulled up behind the Plymouth.

Bogach stared at his bloodstained left arm in total disbelief. The Englishman had merely fired in his general direction, but by a million-to-one chance, the bullet had shattered his elbow. Still dazed, his arm throbbing with pain, he couldn't understand why his Makarov automatic should be lying on the carpet at his feet.

Bending down, he picked it up and moved away from the window. A perfect ambush had ended in disaster and there was nothing he could do now except try to escape. The Soviet Legation in New York would smuggle him out of the country, but first he had to reach the Oldsmobile parked in the sand dunes down by the creek, and that wasn't going to be easy. Step by step, he made it to the landing and then, leaning his right shoulder against the wall, he eased his way down the staircase.

Hedley tried the back door and finding it locked, moved on to the patio. Every pane of glass in the kitchen was still intact and he had a hunch the gunman had picked the lock on the French windows when he'd broken into the house. His back to the wall, he reached across and explored them with his fingers. Digging them into the crevice, he felt the windows give, and pushing them open, he pulled the drawn curtains aside and slipped into the living room.

For a few moments he stood there, waiting for his eyes to become accustomed to the gloom. Then, carefully picking his way between two armchairs covered in dust sheets, he crept toward the door and slowly unlatched it. The woodwork splintered, something struck him a violent blow on the chest, and reeling back, he cannoned into a table and crashed to the floor. The door swung open and somewhere a long way off, he thought he could hear Janet calling to him.

Bogach peered into the living room. He'd seen the latch turn and he knew Hedley had been hit by his snap shot, but he couldn't afford to take any chances. A wounded man was still a dangerous adversary, especially when he was behind you. A blurred shape on the floor caught his eye and smiling to himself, he raised the Makarov, and then a loud, high-pitched voice said, "Freeze."

Janet watched the gunman slowly turn in her direction to face the kitchen window. Leo was still working his way down the far side of the house and she wished to God he would get a move on because she was out of breath from running and it was almost impossible to hold the .32 Colt revolver steady. She stared at the Makarov automatic in his hand, waiting and hoping that the gunman would drop it but instead his finger was tightening on the trigger, and firing rapidly, she emptied all six chambers. Hit in the stomach, chest, and mouth, Bogach fell sideways on to the tiled floor, his face turned toward the freezer.

Kaplin said, "Are you all right, Jan?"

"No," she whispered. "No, I don't mind telling you, Leo, I'm far from all right."

Kaplin removed the Colt revolver from her limp grasp, shoved it into his pocket, and drew her away from the kitchen window. He knew how she felt—sick in the stomach, the mind numb with shock. It had happened to him a long time ago, late at night in a dark alley of a small Belgian village called Trois Pont when the Germans had busted through the Ardennes and he'd shot one of Skorzeny's commandos dressed in American uniform. "You had no choice, Leo," the other guys had told him, but it hadn't made him feel any better about it and he'd quickly discovered that keeping busy was the only way to throw off that initial mood of black depression.

"Why don't you call the chief of police and tell him what's happened here, Jan?" he suggested quietly. "I'll look for Hedley."

"James?" Her eyes went to the open French windows. "He's in there, isn't he?" she said in a dull voice.

"He could be." Kaplin put out a hand to stop her but she brushed it aside and ran into the living room.

Hedley was sprawled on the floor, holding his chest with one hand, his back wedged against an armchair. Blood was seeping through the outspread fingers and she noticed that his face was sallow, the color of old parchment, the cheeks sunken and wet with perspiration.

"Oh God," she murmured and sank down on her knees beside him. Moving his hand away, she opened his jacket and tugging the shirt out of his pants, began to unbutton it. "Oh God," she repeated.

Hedley moistened his lips and looked up at Kaplin. "Upstairs," he croaked, "the bathroom—top shelf of the medicine cabinet—a pawn ticket."

Kaplin stared back at him, an incredulous expression on his face. "Is it important?" he asked.

Hedley nodded. He wanted to tell Kaplin that seven people had died for it but he was desperately tired and it was too much effort.

"Okay," said Kaplin, "I'll get it."

"Like hell you will," Janet said fiercely. "The pawn ticket can wait. Get an ambulance—and fast."

"Right." He didn't move.

"Don't just stand there," she snapped. "Get one." She raised the hem of her dress above her thighs and, grabbing hold of the white lawn half-slip with both hands, ripped off a broad strip.

"You know something?" Hedley whispered. "You've got nice legs." Then he fainted.

1956

Monday, November 19

19.

Winter ignored the glass of brandy in front of him and stared at the gray patch of November sky above the rooftops. Cleaver had been very guarded on the telephone and even now, when they were face to face in his office, he was curiously reluctant to explain why he had wanted him to call around to Leconfield House. Twice he'd seemed on the point of disclosing the reason but on each occasion he'd shied away from it and spoken of other matters, particularly the demonstrations that had been held in Trafalgar Square to protest against the Suez invasion.

"I didn't know we had so many subversives," Cleaver said for the second time. "Believe me, we took enough photographs to keep Special Branch employed for months."

"Is that a fact?" Winter averted his gaze from the window and looked at Cleaver through narrowed eyes. "Now suppose you tell me what is really on your mind."

"Do you want it straight from the shoulder?"

"Why not? You were never one to beat about the bush, Malcolm."

"All right," said Cleaver. "When do you expect them to give you the boot?"

"I'm still answering the phone from the same office."

"That's no answer." Cleaver scowled and leaned forward, elbows resting on the desk, his shoulders hunched. "Three weeks ago you asked me to fix a legend for Hedley and I turned you down."

"Somewhat testily, as I recall," Winter said dryly.

"Maybe so, but how come you got away with it?"

"I didn't have to lift a finger. Hedley gave the CIA the top KGB agent in New York and two sleepers, so they damn well had to cover for him."

There had been other mitigating factors at work that certain Monday morning three weeks ago. Bracecourt had been in an almighty flap, redrafting the Anglo-French ultimatum for the umpteenth time, and in the circumstances, he hadn't wanted to know about Miles. The general too had taken some of the heat out of the situation, letting it be known that he wanted his son buried in the nearest military cemetery. Only Control knew the whole story and Control, being a canny Scot, had decided to wait and see what happened, on the grounds that the government had enough problems to cope with for the time being without him adding to them.

"You've got the luck of the devil," said Cleaver.

The luck of the devil? Not when Katherine was visibly wasting away, dying a little each day. "You're wrong, Malcolm," he said quietly. "I'll be for the chop as soon as the dust settles on the Suez affair."

"I said you had the luck of the devil and I meant it." Cleaver opened a drawer in his desk, took out two glossy photographs, and placed them side by side on the blotting pad. "I don't have to point out which one is Vasili Korznikov, do I?"

Winter stared at each photograph in turn, his pulse quickening. "Where and when were they taken?" he asked in a muted voice.

"The one on the left was taken in Waterlow Park, Highgate, on Guy Fawkes night. You can just see one of the bonfires in the background. The other was shot in Kensington Gardens yesterday morning. Korznikov seems to have a preference for wide-open spaces."

232

"It's standard operating procedure with the KGB."

"Oh, really?" Cleaver smiled. "Well, right now, I think we both owe Lovell a drink."

The name struck a chord. Winter frowned, then recalled that Lovell was the Special Branch officer who had spotted Rida and Korznikov together at the Yugoslavian Embassy. "You're absolutely right, Malcolm. What does he drink?"

"Beer," said Cleaver.

"I'll send him a barrel."

"Good. He can share it with the eight officers who were detailed to keep an eye on Korznikov." Cleaver rubbed his jaw. "The question is: What are we going to do about the rotten apple in your barrel?"

"I'd like to play him for as long as we can."

"Yes, I rather thought you would want to turn him round. That's the Winter touch, isn't it?"

"You could say that." Winter pointed to the photographs. "May I borrow these?" he asked.

"Be my guest," said Cleaver.

Deakin initialed the cable from Head of Station, Budapest, and closed the file. For a while, he'd been tempted to add a few pithy comments of his own but, on reflection, had decided the cable didn't need any embellishments from him. The message from Budapest was crystal clear: the Hungarians felt they had been betrayed by the United Nations, who had preferred to devote all their energies toward saving Nasser's face instead of supporting them in their struggle for freedom. There was also a widespread conviction that the withdrawal of the Soviet Army from Hungary which had started on Monday, October 29, would have continued but for the Anglo-French invasion of Suez.

Although history was full of "ifs" and "buts," Deakin felt the Hungarians had a point. Certainly Khrushchev had become extremely bellicose after the RAF had started bombing the airfields in the Canal Zone, even going so far as to suggest that the U.S. Sixth Fleet should combine forces with the Red Navy to drive the British and French out of Egypt. Not satisfied with that, he'd sent Eden a stiff note asking him how he would like it if his country were to be bombarded with rockets. The government had been unimpressed, their sangfroid bolstered by the knowledge that the Soviets did not possess a single Intermediate Range Ballistic Missile in their armory, but Eisenhower had taken Khrushchev seriously and there had been some wry amusement in Whitehall when it was learned that he'd put the Strategic Air Command on full alert. Even Winter had permitted himself a quiet smile at that.

A loud sneeze interrupted Deakin's train of thought and, glancing to his left, he saw Turnock standing in the open doorway. He looked like death warmed over, his face haggard, his eyes heavy with a bad cold and his nose the color of a ripe tomato.

"You should be at home, Bill," he said, "tucked up in a nice warm bed."

"Impossible, George, I've got too much on." Turnock pulled out a damp handkerchief and blew his nose. "Have you seen Winter this morning?" he asked in a hoarse voice.

"No."

"Strange." Turnock clucked his tongue. "He's not in his office and his PA doesn't seem to know where he's gone."

"There's nothing unusual about that," said Deakin. "Charles can be pretty elusive at times."

"It's important I see him, George. There are some very disquieting reports coming out of Iraq and things don't look too good for Faisal and Nuri-es-Said. It seems there's a great deal of unrest in the army, particularly amongst the junior officers. The name of Brigadier Abdul Karem Kassem keeps cropping up. Ever heard of him?"

"No, I can't say I have."

Turnock frowned and shuffled his feet. Observing him closely, Deakin thought he had good reason to be worried. His sudden volte-face hadn't fooled Winter and he was under a cloud. Since the Suez debacle, there had been some talk that his department was to be split up, the Persian Gulf area becoming a separate entity. Whatever its merits, reorganizing the Arabian Desk was a very neat way of emasculating Turnock.

"Do you think there's anything to these reports, George?"

Information was usually assessed on the proven reliability of the source, but in this instance Deakin thought the normal yardstick irrelevant. Instead of destroying Nasser, Eden had created a folk hero and almost overnight had made him the most powerful leader in the Arab world. Henceforth, people such as Nuri-es-Said, who were obviously pro-Western, would find themselves isolated, and one by one they would fall like overripe fruit from the tree.

"Well, one thing's certain," said Deakin, "true or false, there's nothing we can do about it. The Middle East is no longer our oyster."

"I doubt if Winter will be pleased to hear you say that."

"Take my advice—don't make the point to him."

"Don't worry, I won't."

"I think you're very wise, Bill."

Turnock smiled wryly and backed away. Waiting until he could no longer hear his footsteps in the corridor, Deakin lifted the phone and rang Winter's PA. He had noticed of late that Charles was always in a foul mood after Bill had been to see him and anxious not to catch the backlash on his temper, he thought it advisable to get in first. Somewhat to his surprise, the PA said she was about to ring him and would he please come straight up.

Winter was standing in the window, gazing out across the rooftops, his hands deep in the pockets of the same dark Savile Row pinstripe he'd been wearing the day they'd learned that Hedley had been expelled from Budapest. Deakin glanced at the desk, half expecting to see an open file on the blotting pad, but there was only a large brown envelope, the flap unsealed

"You know something, George?" Winter said, looking at the gray November sky. "I do believe it's going to brighten up."

"Really? According to the forecast I heard, it's going to be dull all day."

"That only goes to show how wrong the weathermen can be."
Winter returned to his desk and sat down. "I understand from
my PA that you've received a very interesting report from
Moscow."

"I'm afraid you've been misinformed, Charles. The cable is
from Head of Station, Budapest."

"I'm quite sure it's Moscow, George." Smiling, Winter extracted the photographs from the envelope and passed them to
Deakin. "I mean, that is Vasili Korznikov you're talking to,
isn't it?"

Deakin stared at the photographs, his mouth open. Presently,
his hands began to tremble. "You . . . " He swallowed nervously and tried again. "You knew all along then?"

Winter shook his head. "No, as a matter of fact, my money
was on Bill Turnock. Right from the day he returned from
Paris, Bill made it very clear that he was dead against us becoming a party to the secret agreement between France and
Israel. At the time, I thought he was pro-Arab but now, having
reviewed his personal records, I've come to realize that he
simply hated the Jews. I have to hand it to you, George, you
were very clever."

"Clever?" Deakin repeated in a hollow voice.

"Well, Turnock was your protégé and I imagine he told you
about the discrepancies he'd found in the Imprest Account.
From then on, you used him as a stalking horse and Bill was
just too stupid to realize what you were doing. You pointed him
toward the Trans Globe Travel Agency, didn't you?"

"Yes." Deakin's voice was barely audible.

"And then, to cover your tracks, you reminded me how Bill
felt about the use of force to resolve the Suez dispute and said
you were afraid that he might do something stupid."

"Why bother to ask?" Deakin said wearily. "You already
know all the answers."

"Not quite." Winter smiled. "Tell me about Alan Squires."

Deakin pushed a hand through his haid. "I met Alan when
I was with the British Middle East Office," he said haltingly,

'and we became good friends. We had a lot in common, same interests, same outlook on life. Anyway, when I realized what you had in mind, he agreed to pass on a timely warning to Aziz Rida at the Egyptian Embassy, and that's how it all started. Rida didn't like dealing with an intermediary and he asked Alan if I would meet him at the Uddenbergs' flat in Sussex Gardens. I said it was too risky."

"You mean you had a better idea," Winter said harshly. "You sent word that the Uddenbergs should invite Turnock to dinner while you and Rida met elsewhere the same night, which is why the Squires gave a cocktail party for you and Marjorie."

Deakin looked shocked. "You had me under surveillance," he said, as if that was an ungentlemanly thing to do.

"You and Bill. Unfortunately, the Special Branch officer was left stranded, high and dry, when you and the Squires drove off. That was a stroke of luck for you, because thereafter we decided that Turnock was our man. Still, the pendulum swung our way in the end." Winter smiled again but without warmth. "You really are a little shit, aren't you, George?"

"You don't understand," Deakin protested.

"Oh, I understand your motives all right. You thought you were acting in the best interests of the country. Eden had lost his marbles and you had to put a stop to the Suez adventure if we were to retain any influence in the Middle East."

"So what happens now?"

"Nothing," said Winter. "You soldier on and draw the usual pension when you retire in ten years' time."

"And?" Deakin whispered.

"And during the next ten years, you'll lead Korznikov and his successors to believe they have penetrated the upper echelons of the SIS. We're going to feed those people in Dzerzhinsky Square with false information until they don't know whether they're coming or going."

There would be other spin-offs. The KGB would ask Deakin for specific information and their questions would be very revealing. Then too, when the time was ripe, he would invite

McNulty to join the game. There would be an entrance fee of course; just how big he had yet to decide but it would be pretty steep.

"What if I were to refuse?" Deakin asked in a monotone.

Winter raised an eyebrow. "I don't think you can, George," he said quietly. "Besides, there's always Hedley. How would you like to meet him one dark night?"

CLIVE EGLETON *was a colonel in the British army until five years ago, when he retired to write full time. He is the author of eight novels besides* THE EISENHOWER DECEPTION, *including* BACKFIRE, THE MILLS BOMB, SKIRMISH, THE BORMANN BRIEF, SEVEN DAYS TO A KILLING (*made into the movie* THE BLACK WINDMILL, *with Michael Caine*), THE JUDAS MANDATE, LAST POST FOR A PARTISAN, *and* A PIECE OF RESISTANCE. *He lives with his family in England.*